ARDUINO PROGRAMMING: 2 BOOKS IN 1

- The Ultimate Beginner's & Intermediate Guide to Learn Arduino Programming Step By Step

RYAN TURNER

© Copyright 2018 - **Ryan Turner** - All rights reserved.

The content contained within this book may not be reproduced, duplicated or transmitted without direct written permission from the author or the publisher.

Under no circumstances will any blame or legal responsibility be held against the publisher, or author, for any damages, reparation, or monetary loss due to the information contained within this book. Either directly or indirectly.

Legal Notice:

This book is copyright protected. This book is only for personal use. You cannot amend, distribute, sell, use, quote or paraphrase any part, or the content within this book, without the consent of the author or publisher.

Disclaimer Notice:

Please note the information contained within this document is for educational and entertainment purposes only. All effort has been executed to present accurate, up to date, and reliable, complete information. No warranties of any kind are declared or implied. Readers acknowledge that the author is not engaging in the rendering of legal, financial, medical or professional advice. The content within this book has been derived from various sources. Please consult a licensed professional before attempting any techniques outlined in this book.

By reading this document, the reader agrees that under no circumstances is the author responsible for any losses, direct or indirect, which are incurred as a result of the use of information contained within this document, including, but not limited to, — errors, omissions, or inaccuracies.

TABLE OF CONTENTS

ARDUINO PROGRAMMING: THE ULTIMATE BEGINNER'S GUIDE TO LEARN ARDUINO PROGRAMMING STEP BY STEP 1

Introduction To Arduino 3
What Is Arduino? 10
   History Of Arduino 10
   But What Is Arduino? 11
   Who Uses Arduino? 12

The 6 Advantages Of Arduino 14
Key Terms In Understanding Arduino 16
   Anatomy Of The Arduino Board 16
   Other Terms About Working With Arduino 18

Understanding The Choices 20
      Uno 20
      Leonardo 21
      101 21
      Esplora 22
      Mega 256o 23
      Zero 24
      Due 25
      Mega Adk 27
      Arduino Pro (8 Mhz) 28
      Arduino Pro (16 Mhz) 29
      Arduino M0 30
      Arduino M0 Pro 30
      Arduino Yún (Based On Atmega32u4) 31
      Arduino Ethernet 32
      Arduino Tian 33
      Industrial 101 34

- Arduino Leonardo Eth 35
- Gemma 36
- Lilypad Arduino Usb 37
- Lilypad Arduino Main Board 38
- Lilypad Arduino Simple 39
- Lilypad Arduino Simple Snap 40
- Other Boards 41

Choosing And Setting Up The Arduino 42
- Choosing A Board 42
- How Many Digital And Analog Pins Will I Require To Have The Functionality That I Desire? 42
- Do I Want This To Be A Wearable Device? 43
- Do I Want To Connect To The Internet Of Things? If So, How? 43
- Getting Started On Arduino Ide 43
- Coding A Program For Your Arduino 45
- Connecting To The Arduino Board 45
- Uploading To The Arduino Board 46
- Running The Arduino With Your Program 47

Coding For The Arduino 49
- Structure 49

Control Structures 50

Syntax 52

Arithmetic Operators 53
Comparison Operators 55
Data Types 58
- Void 58
- Boolean 59
- Char 59
- Unsigned Char 59

- Byte 60
- Int 60
- Unsigned Int 60
- Word 60
- Long 61
- Unsigned Long 61
- Short 61
- Float 62
- Double 62

Turn Your Arduino Into A Machine 63
- Useful Constants 65
- Initialization Of The Serial Port 66
- Initialize The Digital Pin And Switch It Off 66
- Reading The Sensor Temperature 66
- Transfer The Sensor Values To The Pc 67
- Convert The Sensor Reading Into A Voltage 68
- Changing Voltage To Temperature Before Uploading To The Pc 68
- Turn Off The Leds For Low Temperature 68
- Turn On The Led To Create A Low Temperature 70
- To Create A Medium Temperature, Turn On The Two Leds .. 70

C Language Basics And Functions 71
- Memory Maps 72

Logic Statements 73
For Loops 80
Arrays 84
Operators 88
- Arithmetic Operators 88
- Boolean Operators 88

Decision Making 90
- If Statement 90

Inputs, Outputs, And Sensors 94
    Steps 99

Computer Interfacing With An Arduino 111
Catching Up (Revisiting) 123
    Arduino 123
    The Structure Of An Arduino 124
    Foundations Of C Programming 124
    Working With Variables And Values 125
    Assignment And Math 127
    Arrays 129

More In-Depth Computer Science Topics 142
Arduino Api Functions 153
Using The Stream Class (And Working With Strings) 163
User Defined Functions 169
Conclusion 172
References 175

ARDUINO PROGRAMMING: THE ULTIMATE INTERMEDIATE GUIDE TO LEARN ARDUINO PROGRAMMING STEP BY STEP 177

Introduction 179
    How To Benefit The Most 180

Chapter 1: Programming Improvements 181
    Functions 181

        The Benefits Of Functions 184

    Mathematical Functions And Arduino 185

        Trigonometric Functions 186

    Calculation Optimizations 189

- Bit Shift Operations 189
- Lookup Tables 192
  - Application 193
- Time 196

Chapter 2: Digital Inputs 199
- Perceiving The Outside World 199
  - Processing 201
  - Linking The Physical To The Virtual 205
  - The Debounce Concept 213

Chapter 3: Serial Communication 218
- General Aspects 218
  - Serial Communication Types 220
- Multiple Serial Protocols 221

Chapter 4: Visual Output Feedback 225
- Using Leds 225
  - Coupling 227
  - Multiplexing 230
  - Using Random Seeds 232
  - Daisy Chaining 234
- Using Lcds 239

Chapter 5: Movement 243
- Using A Piezoelectric Sensor 243
  - Transistors 246
- Using Servomotors 247
  - Multiple Servomotors 249
  - Stepper Motors 252
- Sound 256

Digitizing Sound	260
Producing Sounds With Arduino	262
Chapter 6: Advanced Techniques	**265**
Improved Data Storage	265
Working With Gps Modules	272
The Parallax Gps Receiver Module	273
Parsing Data	274
Arduino Autonomy	284
Using Batteries	285
Using Power Adaptors	287
Chapter 7: Networking	**290**
Open Systems Interconnection	291
Layers And Protocols	292
Ip Addresses And Ports	294
Using Wired Ethernet	297
Using Bluetooth	306
Conclusion	**318**

ARDUINO PROGRAMMING

The Ultimate Beginner's Guide To Learn Arduino Programming Step By Step

RYAN TURNER

INTRODUCTION TO ARDUINO

In case you've never heard of an Arduino before, it is an open-source electronic interface that has two parts: the first is the programable circuit board, and the other is a coding program of your choice to run to your computer. Arduinos come in many forms, including the Arduino Uno, LilyPad Arduino, Redboard, Arduino Mega, Arduino Leonardo, and others which we will explain later on.

If you're unfamiliar with programming, this is a good place to start. The Arduino can be programmed in various types of programming languages, and its wide array of Arduino options can give you more programming experience. Arduinos come with additional attachments, some in the form of sensors, and others can be obtained anywhere and can be attached to the various ports on an Arduino. Arduino is a great stepping stone on the way to understanding programming and sensor interaction.

In programming languages, there is always the well-known program, "Hello World" that is showcased on the screen. In the microcontroller world that we are in, this phase or first program is indicated by a blinking of the light, "on" and "off" to show that everything you have set up works correctly.

We will look at the sketches in their entirety and explain the details after explaining the code. If you go through something that you cannot make something out of, keep on reading, and it will be clear.

Let us look at this program, to show you how we will be breaking down the codes.

Const int PinkL = 13;

Void setup ()

{ pinMode (PinkL, OUTPUT); }

Void loop ()

{digitalWrite(PinkL, HIGH);

 delay (600);

digitalWrite(PinkL, LOW);

delay(600); }

On the first part

Const int PinkL = 13;

This line is used to define a constant that is used throughout the program to specify a particular value. All pins are recommended to have this because it makes it easy for software change if the circuit is still the same. In programming in Arduino, the constants are commonly named starting with the letter "k".

The second to part

 Void setup ()

{pinMode (PinkL, OUTPUT);}

The OUTPUT is pin 13. This now makes Arduino control the coding to the pins, instead of reading from it.

The third part

```
Void loop()
{digitalWrite (PinkL, HIGH);
delay(600);
digitalWrite(PinkL, LOW);
Delay(600);}
```

This is where the core part of the code is. A HIGH is written to the pin that leads to the turning of the LED. When you place HIGH, it means that 5V is the pin's output. The other option we have is LOW, which means that you are putting 0V out.

A delay() is called to delay the number of milliseconds that is sent to it. Since we send 600, there will be a delay of 0.6 of a second. The LED goes off, and this is attributed to the LOW that is written as an output on the pin.

A 600 milliseconds delay will be activated.

This will be the sequence until the Arduino goes off or the power is disconnected from it.

Before you start digesting more content, try this program out and ensure that it works just fine. To test if you have set your LED in reverse order, the following might happen. On the UNO board, you have pin 13 connected to a Light Emitting Diode connected. When it blinks and the breadboard LED does not blink, then you might have connected your LED in reverse. In case you see that it is blinking once in a second, then the program has not been sent to the Arduino successfully.

When you've completed the programming, place comments in the coding lines to instruct the Arduino. These comments can instruct your Arduino to blink the LED intermittently or through various sequences.

The programs we normally write are usually meant for the computers and not for people to understand once they are opened up. There is a good provision that allows us, humans, to read the program easily and the computer will have no clue about it. There are two comments that are possible in this program:

1. The block comment style starts with two characters, /* which progresses until */ is seen. Multiple lines are then crossed and here are a few examples.

/* This is the first line*/

/* the program was successful*/

/* we

*are

*going

*far */

2. Commenting can be done on a line that has the backslash operator //. This is the part that is meant for humans and not machines. It is another way to insert a comment.

When you add comments in a program, you will have a code that looks like the statement above.

You will find in the following pages, that if there is no number next to the line of code, it indicates a comment continuation from the line at the top. We might not showcase this in perfection because we are using a limited space in our book. You will find a hyphen at the line's end that is continued and a hyphen along the continuation line. This is just our way of handling it, but in an IDE, you won't find it and you need not type them.

```
/*
* Program Name: Blink123
*Author: James Aden
* Date written: 24 July 2017
*Description:
* Turns an LED on for a sixth-hundred of a second, then for another sixth-hundred of a- -second on a continuous repetitive session
*/

/* Pin Definitions */

Const  int PinkL = 13;

/*
*Functions Name: setup
*Purpose: Run once after system power up
*/

Void setup(){pinMode(PinkL,OUTPUT);}

/*

Void    loop(){digitalWrite(PinkL,HIGH);Delay(600);digitalWrite(PinkL,LOW);Delay(600):}
```

Gotchas

If you find out that your program does not compile, or it gives you a different result than what you need, here are a few things that people get confused about:

The programming language is normally sensitive to capitalization of letters. For instance, myVar is considered different to MyVar.

Tabs, blank lines, and white spaces are equivalent to a single space, making it easier for one to read.

Code blocks are normally grouped using curly braces, i.e., "{" and "}"

All open parenthesis have a corresponding closing parenthesis, i.e. "(" and ")"

Numbers don't have commas. So instead of writing 1,000, ensure that you write 1000.

All program statements MUST end with a semicolon. This means that each statement except for the following two cases:

-In comments

- after curly braces are placed "}"

Assignment task to test what you have learned:

1. Alter the delay time of your LED before it comes back on to stick to 1.5 seconds. Leave the ON time of the LED limited to 600 milliseconds.

2. From pin 13, change to pin 2, making it the new connection to the LED. Keep in mind that both the circuit & and the program will be different.

This is just a basis for basic Arduino programming. In the rest of the book, we will be looking at how Arduinos can be programmed with respect to different functions. If you're new to programming, don't let the above codes frighten you. Coding takes practice, but it relatively easy to learn, just like a new language.

WHAT IS ARDUINO?

With the age of technology being in full swing, there is an increase in the average person's technological literacy. More and more people are becoming versed in the hardware and software of the modern age, whether as a dabbling hobbyist or as a professional engineer.

For whatever reason, you and many others have been attracted to Arduino. Perhaps you have seen the variety of projects online or in-person that are built on Arduino technologies, or maybe you have heard of the flexibility and ease of building gadgets with Arduino. Whatever the case, you are interested in learning more about Arduino and how to utilize the technology in your own life. First, let us look at what Arduino is and its history.

History of Arduino

The Arduino technology started as an idea in 2003 by Hernando Barragán to simplify the BASIC stamp microcontroller and reduce costs for non-engineering students to purchase such technology at the Interactive Design Institute in Ivrea, Italy. A microcontroller is a small computer board that can be programmed to perform certain functions. At the time, BASIC stamp microcontrollers cost $100 and upward, and, as we will see later, Arduino certainly reduced the costs while maintaining the ability to perform various functions and the ease of programming such functions.

Supervised by Massimo Banzi and Casey Reas, Barragán worked in the computer language called Processing to create the environment, IDE (Arduino's official coding environment and program). He fiddled with the Wiring platform technology to come up with the hardware called ATmega168, the first Arduino microcontroller.

Later in 2003, Massimo Banzi, David Mellis, and David Cuartielles added support for Wiring to their microcontroller board, named ATmega8, and they reworked the Wiring source code, naming it Arduino. Together, the three along with Tom Igoe and Gianluca Martino continued to develop Arduino technologies, and by the year 2013, 700,000 microcontroller boards were sold from the New York City supplier, Adafruit Industries, alone.

After some issues with establishing the trademark for Arduino, which resulted in a split in the company for a few years, Arduino is now a single company that is committed to the development of hardware and software usable by the average person or hobbyist, but also flexible enough to be of interest to the professional engineer.

But what is Arduino?

This history of Arduino might sound as convoluted as the technology itself seems to you. Full of many puzzling and confusing elements, you might feel overwhelmed by the language of "microcontrollers," "environments," and "languages." However, this book is intended to demystify Arduino. We will start here, beginning with the definition of Arduino.

How it works is as follows: one purchases the hardware that is appropriate to his or her purposes and then, on a more powerful Windows, Macintosh OSX, or Linux computer, and codes or write instructions for the board and uploads the instructions via a cable. The code is then stored on the microcontroller, and it functions according to the instructions, such as activating a beeping sound when light filters in through an opening door. The light activates a sensor connected to the microcontroller, like an alarm.

Who Uses Arduino?

A wide array of people uses Arduino for various projects and hobbies, as well as for professional uses. It is known for being simple and straightforward enough for beginners, deep and rich enough for the beginner to grow, and with enough potential for a more advanced user to utilize.

Teachers and students use Arduino, and indeed are the intended consumer base for the products, as Arduino offers a low-cost way to build scientific instruments. This allows teachers and students to practice and demonstrate chemistry and physics principles, as well as get started with programming and building robots.

Designers and architects might use Arduino technologies to build interactive models and prototypes of what they hope to develop on a full-scale. Musicians and artists also use Arduino microcontrollers to experiment with new instruments or techniques in their art.

Just about anyone can use Arduino, including children, that want to start tinkering with coding and computer hardware, as well as hobbyists who simply want to learn a bit about software and microcomputers.

THE 6 ADVANTAGES OF ARDUINO

- The driving force behind creating Arduino microcontrollers was cost-efficiency. Rather than the $100 that some other boards cost, a pre-assembled Arduino board costs less than $50, and the boards that can be manually put together cost even less.

- The Arduino environment, IDE, works across different platforms. This means that you can use a Windows computer like any other microcontroller board would probably require, but you can also use a Macintosh OSX computer, or a computer running Linux and work just as easily with the Arduino software. This opens up the use of microcontrollers to the Apple user and the open-source Linux user.

- The software for Arduino is open-source. The tools, or strings of code that you use to instruct the microcontroller to accomplish certain functions, are accessible by anyone. You do not have to purchase a license to use these tools so that teachers can teach students about them and students can learn them without added cost.

- The open-source tools are also extendable by the C++ libraries and the AVR-C coding language, meaning that those with more in-depth knowledge of code would be able to benefit from using these technologies as well. There is depth to the software and programming features that allow the more dedicated person to go deeper while being enough of a straightforward coding language to allow the hobbyist to tinker as well.

- The environment in which a person codes for the microcontroller is simple and clear. This means that the computer program, IDE, which you would use to program the instructions for the microcontroller, is straightforward and easy to understand. This makes working with the software a smooth experience.

- The open-source hardware. Arduino board technologies are published under a Creative Commons license. Anyone who desires and has the knowledge to do so could find and create their own hardware to use with Arduino software programming in the IDE environment. Even those who are not experienced circuit designers can use a breadboard to create their own Arduino circuit-board.

KEY TERMS IN UNDERSTANDING ARDUINO

When working with Arduino technologies, it is helpful to understand the terminology of Arduino. You will need to understand the terminology to choose a board, write the coded instructions, set up the microcontroller for use, and finally using the Arduino board. In this chapter, you will find some key terms that will aid you greatly in your endeavor to become an Arduino user.

As mentioned earlier, Arduino is open-source, meaning you can use it and teach it to others without violating any copyright laws. It is based on easy-to-use hardware, which is the actual physical computer board with which you will be working, and straight-forward software, the coded instructions with which you will use to direct the hardware to perform a task of your choosing. The software is also known as code, and the individual pieces of instructions are called tools.

Anatomy of the Arduino Board

The board itself contains a good number of parts. The digital pins run along the edges of most Arduino microcontrollers and are used for input, or sensing of a condition, and output, the response that the controller makes to the input. For example, the input might be that the light sensor senses darkness, that is, a lack of light. It will then close a circuit lighting up a bulb as output: a nightlight for your child.

On most boards, there will be a Pin LED, associated with a specific pin, like Pin 13 on the Arduino Uno. This Pin LED is the only output possibility built into the board, and it will help you with your first project of a "blink sketch," which will be explained later. The Pin LED is also used for debugging or fixing the code you have written so that it has no mistakes in it. The Power LED is what its name implies: it lights up when the board is receiving power or is "turned on." This can also be helpful in debugging your code.

There exists on every board the microcontroller itself, called the ATmega microcontroller, which is the brain of the entire board. It receives your instructions and acts accordingly. Without this, the entire board would have no functionality.

Analog in pins exist on the opposite edge of the board from the digital pins on the Arduino Uno. It is an input into the Arduino system. Analog means that the signal which is input is not constant but instead varies with time, such as audio input. In the example of audio input, the auditory input in a room varies with the people in the room talking and with the noises filtering in from outside the room.

GND and 5V pins are used to create additional power of 5V to the circuit and microcontroller. The power connector is most often on the edge of the Arduino board, and it is used to provide power to the microcontroller when it is not plugged into the USB. The USB port can be used as a power source as well, but its main function is to upload, or transfer, your sketch, or set of instructions that you have coded, from your computer to the Arduino.

TX and RX LED's are used to indicate that there is a transfer of information occurring. This indication of communication will happen when you upload your sketches from your computer to the Arduino so that they will blink rapidly during the exchange.

The reset button is as it sounds: it resets the microcontroller to factory settings and erases any information you have uploaded to the Arduino.

Other Terms about Working with Arduino

There are three types of memory in an Arduino system. Memory is the space where information is stored.

Flash memory is where the code for the program that you have written is stored. It is also called the "program space," because it is used for the program automatically when you upload it to the Arduino. This type of memory remains intact when the power is cut off, or when the Arduino is turned off.

SRAM (static random-access memory) is the space used by the sketch or program you have created to create, store, and work with information from the input sources to create an output. This type of storage disappears once the power is turned off.

EEPROM is like a tiny a hard-drive that allows the programmer to store information other than the program itself when the Arduino is turned off. There are separate instructions for the EEPROM, for reading, writing, and erasing, as well as other functions.

Certain digital pins will be designated as PWM pins, meaning that they can create analog using digital means. Analog, as we remember, means that input (or output) is varied and not constant. Normally, digital pins can only create a constant flow of energy. However, PWM pins can vary the "pulse" of energy between 0 and 5 Volts. Certain tasks that you program can only be carried out by PWM pins.

In addition, in comparing microcontroller boards, you will want to look at clock speed, which is the speed at which the microcontroller operates. The faster the speed, the more responsive it the board will be, but the more battery or energy it will consume as well.

UART measures the number of serial communication lines the device can handle. Serial communication lines are lines that transfer data serially, that is, in a line rather than in parallel or simultaneously. It requires much less hardware to process things serially than in parallel.

Some projects will have you connecting devices to the Internet of Things, which essentially describes the interconnectedness of devices, other than desktop and laptop computers, to various networks in order to share information. Everything from smart refrigerators, to smartphones, to smart TV's are connected to the Internet of Things.

UNDERSTANDING THE CHOICES

Now that we know some basics in understanding the Arduino microcontroller boards let us look at the various options you have when purchasing an Arduino board. We will look at price, functionality, amount of memory, and other features to help make your decision as easy and straightforward as possible.

Uno

This is the board in which most people start their Arduino journey. It is on the smaller side in terms of memory but is very flexible in functionality and a great tool for beginners and those wanting to try their hand and mind at Arduino. This model has a mini-USB port which allows you to upload directly to the board without using a breakout board or other extra hardware.

Price: $24.95

Flash Memory: 32kB

SRAM: 2kB

EEPROM: 1kB

Processing Speed: 16MHz

Digital Pins: 14 pins

PWM Pins: 6 pins

Analog In: 6 pins

Operating Power: 5V

Input Power: 7-12V

Leonardo

The Leonardo microcontroller board is functional out-of-the-box: all you need is a micro-USB cable and a computer to get started. In addition, the computer can recognize the Leonardo as a mouse or a keyboard due to its ATmega32U4 processor.

Price: $19.80

Flash Memory: 32kB

SRAM: 2.5kB

EEPROM: 1kB

Processing Speed: 16MHz

Digital Pins: 20 pins

PWM Pins: 7 pins

Analog In: 12 pins

Operating Power: 5V

Input Power: 7-12V

101

This microcontroller contains a lot of features that are not available in other beginner models. For example, you can connect to the board through Bluetooth Low Energy connectivity from your phone. In addition, it comes with an accelerometer and a gyroscope built in to recognize motion in all directions with its six-axis sensitivity. It can recognize gestures as well.

Put together, these features allow you to have motion of or around the device be the input to which the microcontroller will respond with an output.

Price: $30.00

Flash Memory: 196kB

SRAM: 24kB

EEPROM: 0kB

Processing Speed: 32MHz

Digital Pins: 14 pins

PWM Pins: 4 pins

Analog In: 6 pins

Operating Power: 3.3V

Input Power: 7-12V

Esplora

This board is based on the Leonardo but comes with even more technology built into it so that you do not have to learn as much electronics to get up and running. Instead, you can learn as you see the processes work themselves out.

The input sensors that are built in include a joystick, a slider, a temperature sensor, a microphone, an accelerometer, and a light sensor. It also includes some sound and light outputs. It can expand its capabilities by attaching to other technology called a TFT LCD screen through two Tinker kit input/output connections.

Price: $43.89

Flash Memory:32kB

SRAM: 2.5kB

EEPROM: 1kB

Processing Speed: 16MHz

Digital Pins: n/a

PWM Pins: n/a

Analog In: n/a

Operating Power: 5V

Input Power: 7-12V

Mega 2560

This microcontroller is designed for larger projects like robotics and 3D printers. It has many times the number of digital pins and analog in pins, as well as almost three times the number of PWM pins. This, along with the many times multiplied flash storage,

SRAM, and EEPROM allows for projects that require more instructions. There is space for greater complexity and specificity in this Arduino board.

Price: $45.95

Flash Memory: 256kB

SRAM: 8kB

EEPROM: 4kB

Processing Speed: 16MHz

Digital Pins: 54 pins

PWM Pins: 15 pins

Analog In: 16 pins

Operating Power: 5V

Input Power: 7-12V

UART: 4 lines

Zero

This is an extension of the Arduino Uno technologies that were developed. It is a 32-bit extension of Uno, and it increases performance with a vastly increased processing speed, 16 times the amount of SRAM and a many times multiplied flash memory. You will pay for the extensions, at almost twice the price of the Uno, but you much more than double your capabilities with this hardware.

One other advantage of the Zero is that it has a built-in feature called Atmel's Embedded Debugger, abbreviated as EDBG, which helps you debug your code without using extra hardware and thereby increases your efficiency in the software coding.

Price: $42.90

Flash Memory: 256kB

SRAM: 32kB

EEPROM: n/a

Processing Speed: 48MHz

Digital Pins: 14 pins

PWM Pins: 10 pins

Analog In: 6 pins

Analog Out: 1 pin

Operating Power: 3.3V

Input Power: 7-12V

UART: 2 lines

USB port: 2 micro-USB ports

Due

This is a novelty in the microcontroller board world because it is built on a 32-bit ARM core microcontroller, giving it a great deal of power and functionality. It has an extremely quick processor and 4 UART's, giving it a lot of flexibility and availability to perform multiple functions. It is used for larger scale Arduino projects, and while it might not be your first board, you would do well to consider it for any bigger projects you have down the line.

Price: $37.40

Flash Memory: 512kB

SRAM: 96kB

EEPROM: n/a

Processing Speed: 84MHz

Digital Pins: 54 pins

PWM Pins: 12 pins

Analog In: 12 pins

Analog Out: 2 pins

Operating Power: 3.3V

Input Power: 7-12V

UART: 4 lines

USB ports: 2 micro-USB ports

Mega ADK

This is based on the Mega256O Arduino board, with incredible memory capacity and a lot of availability for input and output. The difference between the Mega256O and the Mega ADK is that the Mega ADK is compatible specifically with Android technologies, such as Samsung phones and tablets, Asus technologies, and other non-iOS, non-Windows, mobile devices that use Android. It comes at a hefty almost $50 price tag, but if you are looking to incorporate Android into your project, this would be the board with which you would want to do so.

Price: $47.30

Flash Memory: 256kB

SRAM: 8kB

EEPROM: 4kB

Processing Speed: 16MHz

Digital Pins: 54 pins

PWM Pins: 15 pins

Analog In: 16 pins

Operating Power: 5V

Input Power: 7-12V

UART: 4 lines

Arduino Pro (8 MHz)

This is the SparkFun company's take on the ATmega328 board. It is basically the Uno for professionals and is meant to be semi-permanent in installation of an object or technology. The 8MHz version is less powerful than the Uno by half, but it is also a good deal cheaper. It requires more knowledge of hardware to get this one working, as it does not have a USB port or a way to power the board by USB, and thus must have a connection to an FTDI cable or breakout board to communicate with the board and upload sketches. Once you get through the technicalities of getting this board hooked up to your computer, however, it functions like a half-power Uno. Unlike the 16MHz Arduino Pro, this 8MHz Pro can be powered by a lithium battery.

Price: $14.95

Flash Memory: 16kB

SRAM: 1kB

EEPROM: 0.512kB

Processing Speed: 8MHz

Digital Pins: 14 pins

PWM Pins: 6 pins

Analog In: 6 pins

Operating Power: 3.3V

Input Power: 3.35-12V

UART: 1 line

Arduino Pro (16 MHz)

This is the 16MHz version of the Arduino Pro by SparkFun. It is the same amount of power as the Uno but has the same drawbacks as the 8MHz Pro: you will need to find an FTDI cable or purchase a breakout board from SparkFun in order to make the board compatible with your computer to upload sketches. This means learning a *bit* more about the technology than if you were to start with the Uno, but after getting things set up, this will function the same as the Uno.

Price: $14.95

Flash Memory: 32kB

SRAM: 2kB

EEPROM: 1kB

Processing Speed: 16MHz

Digital Pins: 14 pins

PWM Pins: 6 pins

Analog In: 6 pins

Operating Power: 5V

Input Power: 5-12V

UART: 1 line

Arduino M0

This board is an extension of Arduino Uno, giving the Uno the 32-bit power of an ARM Cortex M0 core. This will not be your first board, but it might be your most exciting project. It will allow a creative mind to develop wearable technology, make objects with high tech automation, create yet-unseen robotics, come up with new ideas for the Internet of Things, or many other fantastic projects. This is a powerful extension of the straightforward technology of the Uno, and thus it has the flexibility to become almost anything you could imagine.

Price: $22.00

Flash Memory: 256 kB

SRAM: 32kB

Processing Speed: 48MHz

Digital Pins: 20 pins

PWM Pins: 12 pins

Analog In: 6 pins

Operating Power: 3.3V

Input Power: 5-15V

Arduino M0 Pro

This is the same extended technology of the Uno as the Arduino M0, but it has the added functionality and capability of debugging its own software with the Atmel's Embedded Debugger

(EDBG) integrated into the board itself. This creates an interface with the board in which you can debug, or, in other words, a way to interact with the board where you can find the problems in the code you have provided and fix the issues.

Price: $42.90

Flash Memory: 256 kB

SRAM: 32kB

Processing Speed: 48MHz

Digital Pins: 20 pins

PWM Pins: 12 pins

Analog In: 6 pins

Operating Power: 3.3V

Input Power: 5-15V

Arduino YÚN (based on ATmega32U4)

The Arduino YÚN is a great board to use when connecting to the Internet of Things. It is perfect for if you want to design a device connected to a network, like the Internet or a data network. It has built-in ethernet support, which would give you a wired connection to a network, and Wi-Fi capabilities, allowing you to connect cordlessly to the Internet. The YÚN has a processor that supports Linux code in the operating system, or code language, of Linino OS. This gives it extra power and capabilities but retains the ease of use of Arduino.

Price: $68.20

Flash Memory: 32kB

SRAM: 2.5kB

EEPROM: 1kB

Processing Speed: 16MHz

Digital Pins: 20 pins

PWM Pins: 7 pins

Analog In: 12 pins

Operating Power: 5V

UART: 1 line

Arduino Ethernet

This Arduino board is based on the ATmega328, the same microcontroller as the Arduino Uno. Pins 10 through 13 are reserved for interacting with Ethernet, and as such, this board has less input/output capability than the Uno and other Arduino microcontroller boards. It does not connect via USB, but rather through the Ethernet cord, which has the option also to power the microcontroller. There exists on this board, unlike other boards, the option to expand storage through a microSD card reader. The method in which you upload your sketches to this board is similar to the Arduino Pro, and that is via an FTDI USB cable or through an FTDI breakout board. This Arduino model is more complex than a lot of the boards at which we have taken a look, but it has functionalities that are not possible on other boards as well.

Price: $43.89

Flash Memory: 32kB

SRAM: 2kB

EEPROM: 1kB

Processing Speed: 16MHz

Digital Pins: 14 pins

PWM Pins: 4 pins

Analog In: 6 pins

Operating Power: 5V

Input Power: 7-12V

Arduino Tian

The Tian is a miniature computer, with a built-in microprocessor on top of the microcontroller. It has Wi-Fi capabilities like the Arduino YÚN as well as the ethernet capabilities of the YÚN and the Ethernet models. You pay a costly price for the increased functionality and power, but it is many times worth what you pay. This is a fast processor, at 560 MHz clock speed, and on top of it all, this has Bluetooth capabilities. This board also uses the Linino OS, based on the Linux operating system and on OpenWRT.

Price: $95.70

Flash Memory: 256kB (+16MB flash from the microprocessor + 4GB eMMC from the microprocessor)

SRAM: 32kB (+64MB DDR2 RAM from microprocessor)

Processing Speed: 48MHz (560 MHz on the microprocessor)

Digital Pins: 20 pins

Analog In: 6 pins

Operating Power: 3.3V

Input Power: 5V

Industrial 101

The Industrial 101 is essentially a small, less capable YÚN for a little more than half the price. It is intended for "product integration," or, in other words, is meant to be used in long-standing projects. It is intended to function in a semi-permanent role within whatever you are building. The board has built-in Wi-Fi capabilities, a USB connection port, and one Ethernet port by which you can connect to networks via Ethernet cord. This board can be connected to your computer via micro-USB in order to upload your sketches for programming.

Price: $38.50

Flash Memory: 16MB on the processor

SRAM: 2.5KB (RAM is 64 MB DDR2 on the processor)

EEPROM: 1kB

Processing Speed: 16MHz (400MHz for the processor)

Digital Pins: 20 pins

PWM Pins: 7 pins

Analog In: 12 pins

Operating Power: 3.3V

Input Power: 5V

Arduino Leonardo ETH

This is the Arduino Leonardo microcontroller board with an Ethernet port to allow the project to extend to the Internet of Things. You can use the Internet to control the sensors in this way, using your own device as a server or signal provider, or as a client, communicating with the microcontroller to receive instructions. This also contains a micro-USB connector to upload your sketches to the flash memory on the Leonardo ETH. This eliminates the need for a breakout board or TKDI cable. Like the Ethernet model of Arduino, this has the option to be powered by the Ethernet cable as well. There is an onboard microSD card reader for extra storage as well. Essentially, this is a powered-up Leonardo, with greater flexibility to be used in a wider variety of projects and the capacity to be connected to the Internet of Things.

Price: $43.89

Flash Memory: 32kB (4kB is used by the bootloader, so only 28K available for use)

SRAM: 2.5kB

Processing Speed: 16MHz

Digital Pins: 20 pins

PWM Pins: 7 pins

Analog In: 12 pins

Operating Power: 5V

Input Power: 7-12V

Gemma

This Arduino is made by Adafruit Technologies in the USA. The Arduino Gemma is a miniature microcontroller board that is intended to be worn. It indeed has less space and room for functionality than the non-wearable boards, but for many wearable projects, you will not need the robustness of some of the other Arduino microcontroller boards. There is a micro-USB connection on this board, so you do not need a breakout board or TKDI cable. Instead, you simply upload a sketch via the micr0-USB connection and then power the microcontroller by micro-USB or by battery connection.

Price: $9.95

Flash Memory: 8kB

SRAM: 0.5kB

EEPROM: 0.5kB

Processing Speed: 8MHz

Digital Pins: 3 pins

PWM Pins: 2 pins

Analog In: 1 pin

Operating Power: 3.3V

Input Power: 4-16V

Lilypad Arduino USB

This board is round and based on the ATmega32u4 Arduino microcontroller. It contains a micro-USB connected for ease of uploading sketches and for powering the board. There is also a JST connection built in so that, should you decide to power the board by battery, you can do so by connecting a 3.7V Lithium Polymer battery. The difference between the Lilypad Arduino USB and the rest of the Lilypad Arduino models is that the USB model contains the micro-USB port standard, eliminating the need for a breakout board or TKDI adapter. In addition, the board can be seen as a mouse or a keyboard by the computer, among other things.

This board is intended to be worn, like the Gemma. It can be sewn into clothing or otherwise attached to one's body to perform whatever function you have programmed it to perform.

Price: $24.95 (available on SparkFun)

Flash Memory: 32kB

SRAM: 2.5kB

EEPROM: 1kB

Processing Speed: 8MHz

Digital Pins: 9 pins

PWM Pins: 4 pins

Analog In: 4 pins

Operating Power: 3.3V

Input Power: 3.8-5V

Lilypad Arduino Main Board

This is another wearable Arduino microcontroller board. It can be sewn into a piece of fabric or combined with other sensors, actuators, and a power supply to be something you carry with you with the functionality you have programmed yourself. It requires a breakout board and TKDI cable to upload your sketch to the microcontroller's flash memory, but once you have that piece taken care of, you have an inexpensive, wearable device that you have created yourself.

Price: $19.95 (available on SparkFun)

Flash Memory: 16kB (2kB are used by the bootloader so only 14kB are available for use by the programmer)

SRAM: 1kB

EEPROM: 0.512kB

Processing Speed: 8MHz

Digital Pins: 14 pins

PWM Pins: 6 pins

Analog In: 6 pins

Operating Power: 2.7-5.5V

Input Power: 2.7-5.5V

Lilypad Arduino Simple

This Arduino microcontroller board model differs from the Lilypad Arduino Main Board in that it possesses only 9 digital input/output pins, about 2/3 the number of pins on the Main Board. This is a good board for simpler projects that do not require as many inputs and outputs. It is also more powerful than the Main Board, having twice the flash memory, SRAM, and EEPROM. This is a powerful, but less functional version of the Lilypad Arduino Main Board meant to be worn as a transportable device.

Price: $19.95 (available on SparkFun)

Flash Memory: 32kB

SRAM: 2kB

EEPROM: 1kB

Processing Speed: 8MHz

Digital Pins: 9 pins

PWM Pins: 5 pins

Analog In: 4 pins

Operating Power: 2.7-5.5V

Input Power: 2.7-5.5V

Lilypad Arduino Simple Snap

This is a more expensive version of the Lilypad Arduino Simple and is also designed to create wearable devices and e-textiles. It solves an essential problem of the previous versions: washing the textiles in which is it embedded. With the other models of Lilypad Arduino and with the Gemma, one removes the power source and then hand washes the material in which the microcontroller is embedded or sewn. Then, one must wait for the entire circuity to dry before powering back up, or else a short can happen and ruin the technology.

With the Lilypad Arduino Simple Snap, the 9 pins for input/output are snappable buttons such that the microcontroller board can be removed from the material to which it is initially attached. Then, the material can be washed, and the board is returned to its home on the fabric.

The Lilypad Arduino Simple Snap also has a built-in lithium polymer battery (LiPo battery), which can be recharged by attaching power to the charging circuit. The way this board is designed, it has the advantage of being able to detach and attach to a new project.

Price: $29.95 (available on SparkFun)

Flash Memory: 32kB

SRAM: 2kB

EEPROM: 1kB

Processing Speed: 8MHz

Digital Pins: 9 pins

PWM Pins: 5 pins

Analog In: 4 pins

Operating Power: 2.7-5.5V

Input Power: 2.7-5.5V

Other Boards

There exist other boards, like the Arduino Mini, the Pro Mini, the Arduino Robot Control, the Arduino Robot Motor, the Arduino BT, and many others, with the number of options growing quickly.

If you're a beginner, it is recommended that you start with a basic board such as the UNO. Once you're ready for some more advanced projects, these other models might be something you'd like to investigate further! Choosing your Arduino board depends on both the function and convenience of each board. As mentioned above, the UNO is generally considered the board for beginners, but consider how voltage, current, and resistance plays a part in your selections. The inputting power for each project depends on how you will use the board.

For now, let us discover how to get started with Arduino.

CHOOSING AND SETTING UP THE ARDUINO

The first step in setting up your Arduino microcontroller will be to choose an Arduino board with which you want to work.

Choosing a Board

When looking at the options for Arduino Boards, there are a few factors you will want to consider before making a choice. Before deciding on a board, ask yourself the following questions:

How much power do I need to run the application I have in mind?

You might not know the exact measure of flash memory and processing power that you require for your project, but there is a clear difference between the functioning of a simple nightlight that changes colors and a robotic hand with many moving parts. The latter would require a more robust Arduino microcontroller board, with faster processing, more flash memory, and more SRAM than the more straightforward night light idea.

How many digital and analog pins will I require to have the functionality that I desire?

Again, you don't need to have an extremely specific idea in mind but knowing whether you need more pins or less will have a great effect on which board you choose. If you are going for a simple first project, you could get away with having less digital, PWM, and analog pins, while if you are looking to do something more complex, you will want to consider the boards with a great number of pins in general.

Do I want this to be a wearable device?

There are a few options for wearable devices so, of course, this question will not entirely make the decision for you. It will, however, help narrow down the choices and steer you in a direction, with Lilypads and the Gemma or other comparable technologies being your best options.

Do I want to connect to the Internet of Things? If so, how?

If you want connectivity to the Internet of Things, your work will be made much easier by the YÚN, the Tian, the Ethernet, the Leonardo ETH, or the Industrial 101. These have the capabilities of Ethernet connection as well as Wi-Fi capability so you will be able to connect to a network like the Internet and share data or interact with and control other devices on the Internet of Things.

Getting Started on Arduino IDE

The Arduino Software runs in an environment called IDE. This means that you will either need to download the desktop IDE to code in or code online on the online IDE.

The first way that you might access IDE, downloading the desktop application, has a few options to suit the various devices that you might be using. First, there is the Windows desktop application. You can also access it from a Windows tablet or Windows phone with the Windows application. Next, there is the Macintosh OSX version, which allows IDE to run on Apple laptops and desktops, but not on Apple mobile devices like iPhones and iPads. Finally, there are three options for running Arduino IDE on Linux: the 32-bit, the 64-bit, and the Linux ARM version. If you prefer this option to the web browser option, you will simply need to visit the Arduino IDE site by heading to https://www.arduino.cc/en/Main/Software

There, you can download the appropriate version of desktop IDE. Next, you will run the installation application, click through the options presented, and you should have a running Arduino IDE environment in just a few minutes.

This allows you to access the IDE software from Android devices and Apple mobile devices as well since it is based in a web browser that runs on its own platform rather than on the Android or iOS platforms. You can also run the web browser on various computer types, including Linux, Microsoft Windows, and Apple Macintosh. This will allow you to upload your sketches to the Cloud, that is, to store the information you have coded in a secure location that you can then re-access from another device by connection to the Internet.

Coding a Program for Your Arduino

Next you will write code for a program that you want the Arduino board to run. We will cover how to write code for the Arduino boards in the next chapter, but for now let us be sure to understand that the code is written in the IDE on the computer, tablet, or phone, in either the desktop application or the web application. This allows you to see the entire code at once, allowing for easier debugging, or removing of errors.

Once you write the code, you will want to run it and troubleshoot or debug any errors that you find. You will best be able to do this by applying the coded program to the Arduino board and seeing if it runs. To do this, you will need to proceed to the next step of uploading your sketch.

Connecting to the Arduino Board

Some of the boards come with built-in USB, mini-USB, or micro-USB ports. Examples would be the Uno and the Leonardo, for the more beginning stages of your Arduino career. Simply insert the appropriate end of the USB cord into your computer and the other end into the particular USB port that is present on the board you possess, and the Arduino IDE software should recognize the type of board it is. If it does not, you can always choose the correct board from a dropdown menu.

Sometimes you will need to use a TKDI cable or a breakout board in order to make the Arduino compatible with your computer. This means you will insert the TKDI into the TKDI port on the Arduino microcontroller board and then connect it either to your computer or to another board. If you connect the TKDI cable to a breakout board, you will do as you did with the USB-compatible boards: insert the appropriate end of the cord to the breakout board and the other end to the computer. Again, the computer's Arduino IDE software program should recognize your Arduino board, but you can always choose from a dropdown menu should it fail to recognize it.

Uploading to the Arduino Board

To upload your sketch, the program you just created in code, you will need to select the correct board and port to which you would like to upload. It should be easy enough to select the correct board, as you simply look for the board title that matches the name of the type of board you are using.

To select the correct serial port, the options you might choose are as follows:

Mac

Use */dev/tty.usbmodem241* for the Uno, Mega2560 or Leonardo.

Use */dev/tty.usbserial-1B1* for Duemilanove or earlier Arduino boards.

Use */dev/tty.USA19QW1b1P1.1* for anything else connected by a USB-to-serial adapter.

Windows

Use *COM1* or *COM2* for a serial board.

Use *COM4*, *COM5*, or *COM7* or higher for a USB-connected board.

Look in Windows Device Manager to determine which port the device you are using is utilizing.

Linux

Use */dev/ttyACMx* for a serial port.

Use */dev/ttyUSBx* or something like it for a USB port.

Once you have selected the correct board and port, click *Upload* and choose which Sketch to upload from the menu that appears. If you have a newer Arduino board, you will be able to upload the new sketch simply, but with the older boards, you must reset the board before uploading a new sketch, else you will have two, possibly conflicting sketches present in the board's memory, causing it to crash.

Running the Arduino with Your Program

There are a few ways to power your Arduino once you have uploaded the program that you have coded to it. First, you can power it by the USB connection to another powered device, such as your computer. Second, you can power by Ethernet on boards with that capability. This means that by connecting to the network, you will be connected to a power source through the Ethernet. Finally, you can power most Arduino's by lithium polymer battery.

Once power is connected, and the specified input is put into the microcontroller, it will perform the function for which it is intended.

CODING FOR THE ARDUINO

Coding a program for Arduino means learning a new language, but it is not as hard as you might think. In the same way that mathematics has its own set of symbols to denote various functions like addition, subtraction, and multiplication, there are different symbols and terms used when coding for Arduino. If you have had experience working with coding in the past, learning a new language is easy. For those of you who have never learned to code, translating one form of code to another is like translating one language to another. Though this may seem difficult, the idea of coding is to make coding for other programs easier in the future. Below is a list of the terms and words that are used in Arduino IDE coding and how to use them.

Structure

setup()

This is the function called on when the sketch starts and will run only once after startup or reset. You can use it to start variables, pin modes, or the use of libraries (specific terms you can download for extra functionality).

loop()

The loop function requires the Arduino microcontroller board to repeat a function multiple times, continuously or until a certain variable or condition is met. You will set the condition for it to stop the loop or you will have it loop continuously until you detach the Arduino from the power source or turn it off.

CONTROL STRUCTURES

Control structures show how an input will be received. Just like the name implies, various inputs regarding control determine how your data will be read. Provisional language will also be considered in data analysis. Popular and various control structures are mentioned below.

If

This is what links a condition or input to an output. It means that *if* a certain condition has been met, a specific output or response of the microcontroller will occur. For example, *if* the thermometer to which the microcontroller is attached measures more than 75 degrees Fahrenheit, you might write the code to direct the Arduino to send a signal to your air conditioning unit to turn on to decrease the temperature back to 75 degrees.

If...Else

This is like the *If* conditional, but it specifies another action that the microcontroller will take if the condition for the first action is not met. This gives you an option of performing two different actions in two different circumstances with one piece of code.

While

This is a loop that will continue indefinitely until the expression to which it is connected becomes false. That is, it would perform a function until a parameter is met and the statement that set as the condition is made false.

Do... While

This is like the *while* statement, but it always runs at least once because it tests the variable at the end of the function rather than at the beginning.

Break

This is an emergency exit of sorts from a function of the microcontroller. It is used to exit a *do*, *for*, or *while* loop without meeting the condition that must be met to exit that part of the functionality.

Continue

Return

This is the way to stop a function, and it returns a value with which the function terminated to the calling function or the function that is asking for the information.

Goto

This piece of code tells the microcontroller to move to another place, not consecutive, in the coded program. It transfers the flow to another place in the program. Its use is generally discouraged by C language programmers, but it can definitely simplify a program.

SYNTAX

; (semicolon)

This is used as a period in the English language: it ends a statement. Be sure, however, that the statement closed by the semicolon is complete, or else your code will not function properly.

{} (curly braces)

These have many complex functions, but the thing you must know is that when you insert a beginning curly brace, you *must* follow it with an ending curly brace. This is called keeping the braces balanced and is vital to getting your program working.

// (single-line comment)

If you would like to remind yourself or tell others something about how your code functions, use this code to begin the comment and make sure that it only takes up one line. This will not transfer to the processor of the microcontroller but rather will live in the code and be a reference to you and anyone who is reading the code manually.

/* */ (multi-line comment)

This type of comment is opened by the /*, and it spans more than one line. It can itself contain a single line comment but cannot contain another multi-line comment. Be sure to close the comment with */ or else the rest of your code will be considered a comment and not implemented.

#define

This defines a certain variable as a constant value. It gives a name to that value as a sort of shorthand for that value. These do not take up any memory space on the chip so they can be useful in conserving space. Once the code is compiled or taken together as a program, the compiler will replace any instance of the constant as the value that is used to define it.

NOTE: This statement does NOT use a semicolon at the end.

#include

This is used to include other libraries in your sketch, that is, to include other words and coding language in your sketch that would not otherwise be included. For example, you could include AVR C libraries or many tools, or pieces of code, from the various C libraries.

NOTE: Do NOT add the semicolon at the end of this statement, just as you would exclude it from the *#define* statement. If you do include a semicolon to close the statement, you will receive error messages and the program will not work.

ARITHMETIC OPERATORS

Just as the name implies, arithmetic operators complete codes through use of mathematical symbols. Each symbol connects one line of code to another. When looking for an output resulting in measured values, be sure to check your Arduino setup. Connecting wire with Arduino in the wrong voltage receptors may lead to negative or irrelevant values.

= (assignment operator)

This assigns a value to a variable and replaces the variable with the assigned value throughout the operation in which it appears. This is different than == which evaluates whether two variables or a variable and a set value are equal. The double equal signs function more like the single equal sign in mathematics and algebra than the single equal sign in the Arduino IDE.

+ (addition)

This does what you might expect it would do: it adds two values, or the value to a variable, or two to a fixed constant. One thing that you must take into account is that there is a maximum for variable values in the C programming languages. This means that, if your variable maxes out at 32,767, then adding 1 to the variable will give you a negative result, -32,768. If you expect that the values will be greater than the absolute maximum value allowable, you can still perform the operations, but you will have to instruct the microcontroller what to do in the case of negative results. In addition, as well as in subtraction, multiplication, and division, you place the resulting variable on the left and the operation to the right of the = or ==.

Also, another thing to keep in mind is that whatever type of data you input into the operation will determine the type of data that is output by the operation. We will look at types of data later, but for example, if you input integers, which are whole numbers, you will receive an answer rounded to the nearest whole number.

- (subtraction)

This operation, like the addition sign, does what you would expect: it subtracts two values from each other, whether they both are variables, or one is a constant value. Again, you will have to watch out for values greater than the maximum integer value. Remember to place the resulting variable on the left of the equal sign or signs, and the operation on the right.

* (multiplication)

With multiplication especially, you will need to be careful to define what happens if the value you receive from the operation is greater than the greatest allowable value of a piece of data. This is because multiplication especially grows numbers to large, large values.

/ (division)

Remember to place the resulting variable on the left of the operation, and the values that you are dividing on the right side of the operation.

% (modulo)

This operation gives you the remainder when an integer is divided by another integer. For example, if you did $y = 7 \% 5$, the result for y would be 2, since five goes into seven once and leaves a remainder of 2. Remember, you must use integer values for this type of operation.

COMPARISON OPERATORS

Comparison operators compare the values from the left side of the equation to the right. If the left operator does not have the same units as the right, it is still possible to use these operators, but the results may be unpredictable (Arduino.cc).

== (equal to)

This operator checks to see if the data on the left side of the double equal signs match the data on the right side, that is, whether they are equal. For example, you might ask the pin attached to the temperature gauge $t == 75$, and if the temperature is exactly 75 degrees, then the microcontroller will perform a certain task, whether it be turning off the heating or cooling, or turning off a fan.

!= (not equal to)

This is the mirror image of the previous operation. You could just as easily write a program to test $t != 75$ and set up the microcontroller to turn on a heating lamp, turn on a fan, or ignite the wood in the fireplace if this statement is true. Between $==$ and $!=$, you can cover all the possible conditions that input might give your microcontroller.

< (less than)

If this statement is true, then you can program a certain response from your microcontroller, or, in other words, program output for such input.

> (greater than)

INPUT

In the input state, a digital pin will require very little of the processing power and energy from the microcontroller and battery. Instead, it is simply measuring and indicating to the microcontroller its measurements.

OUTPUT

These are very good at powering LED's because they are in a low-impedance state, meaning they let the energy flow freely through them without much resistance. Output pins take their directions from the microcontroller once it has processed the information given by the input pins, and the output pins power whatever mechanism will perform the intended task.

INPUT_PULLUP

This is what mode you will want to use when connected to a button or a switch. There is a lot of resistance involved in the INPUT_PULLUP state. This means that it is best used for Boolean-like situations, such as a switch either being on or off. When there are only two states and not much in between, use INPUT_PULLUP.

LED_BUILTTIN

true

In a Boolean sense, any integer that is not zero is true. One is true, 200 is true, -3 is true, etc. This would be the case when a statement matches reality. One of your pins might be testing a value, and the statement is trying to match *y != 35*, so if the pin receives information that the value of *y* is 25, then the statement *25 != 35* is true.

false

This is part of a Boolean Constant, meaning that a statement is false, or that its logic does not match reality. For example, you could have a statement, *x > 7* and the value the microcontroller receives for x is 3. This would make the statement *false*. It would then be defined as 0 (zero).

integer constants

These are constants that are used by the sketch directly and are in base 10 form, or integer form. You can change the form that the integer constants are written in by preceding the integer with a special notation signifying binary notation (base 2), the octal notation (base 8), or hexadecimal notation (base 16), for example.

floating point constants

These save space in the program by creating a shorthand for a long number in scientific notation. Each time the floating-point constant appears, it is evaluated at the value that you dictate in your code.

DATA TYPES

Data types refer to the type of data received in each of the programming setups you apply. Data received by Arduino are sent to your program of choice to determine various outcomes. Some examples are listed below.

Void

This is used in a function declaration to tell the microcontroller that no information is expected to be returned with this function. For example, you would use it with the *setup()* or *loop()* functions.

Boolean

Boolean data holds one of two values: true or false. This could be true of any of the arithmetic operator functions or of other functions. You will use *&&* if you want two conditions to be true simultaneously for the Boolean to be true, || if you want one of two conditions to be met, either one setting off the output response, and ! for not true, meaning that if the operator is *not* true, then the Boolean is true.

Char

This is a character, such as a letter. It also has a numeric value, such that you can perform arithmetic functions on letters and characters. If you want to use characters literally, you will use a single quote for a single character, *'A'* and a double quote for multiple characters, *"ABC"* such that all characters are enclosed in quotes. This means the microcontroller will output these characters verbatim if the given conditions are met. The numbers -128 to 127 are used to signify various signed characters.

Unsigned Char

This is the same as a character but uses the numbers 0 to 255 to signify characters instead of the "signed" characters which include negatives. This is the same as the byte datatype.

Byte

This type of data stores a number from 0 to 255 in an 8-bit system of binary numbers. For example, B10010 is the number 18, because this uses a base 2 system.

Int

Integers are how you will store numbers for the most part. Because most Arduinos have a 16-bit system, the minimum value is -32,768 and the maximum value of an integer is 32,767. The Arduino Due and a few other boards work on a 32-bit system, and thus can carry integers ranging from -2,147,483,648 to 2,147,483,647. Remember these numbers when you are attempting arithmetic with your program, as any numbers higher or lower than these values will cause errors in your code.

Unsigned Int

This yields the ability to store numbers from 0 to 65,535 on the 8-bit boards with which you will likely be working. If you have higher values than the signed integers will allow, you can switch to unsigned integers and achieve the same amount of range but all in the positive realm, such that you have a higher absolute value of the range.

Word

A word stores a 16-bit unsigned number on the Uno and on other boards with which you will likely be working. In using the Due and the Zero, you will be storing 32-bit numbers using words. Word is essentially the means by which integers and numbers are stored.

Long

If you need to store longer numbers, you can access 4-byte storage, or 32-bit storage in other words, using the long variable. You simply follow an integer in your coded math with the capital letter *L*. This will achieve numbers from -2,147,483,648 to 2,147,483,647.

Unsigned Long

The way to achieve the largest numbers possible and store the largest integers possible is to direct the microcontroller using the unsigned long variables. This also gives you 32 bits or 4 bytes to work with, but being unassigned the 32nd bit is freed from indicating the positive or negative sign in order to give you access to numbers from 0 to 4,294,967,295.

Short

This is simply another way of indicating a 16-bit datatype. On every type of Arduino, you can use short to indicate you are expecting or using integers from -32,768 to 32,767. This helps free up space on your Due or Zero by not wasting space on 0's for a small number and by halving the number of bits used to store that number.

Float

A float number is a single digit followed by 6 to 7 decimal places, multiplied by 10 to a power up to 38. This can be used to store more precise numbers or just larger numbers. Float numbers take a lot more processing power to calculate and work with, and they only have 6 to 7 decimals of precision, so they are not useful in all cases. Many programmers actually try to convert as much float math to integer math as possible to speed up the processing. In addition, these take 32 bits to store versus the normal 16 bits, so if you're running low on storage, try converting your float numbers to integers.

Double

This is only truly relevant to the Due, in which doubling allows for double the precision of a float number. For all other Arduino boards, the floating-point number always takes up 32 bits, so floating does nothing to increase precision or accuracy.

TURN YOUR ARDUINO INTO A MACHINE

While switches and buttons are an excellent thing, still there is a lot more to do than turn it on and off. Although Arduino is a digital device, it can receive information from an analog sensor so that it can measure light, temperature and so on. Various inputs and programming languages give different results, so the outputs are dependent on coding and the sensors you choose. To find more sensors, visit the Arduino website. To create this, you use the built Analog-to-Digital Converter of the Arduino.

You will use a temperature sensor to determine the warmth of your skin. This device releases a changing voltage based on the temperature it detects. It comes with three pins: the first pin connects to the ground while the other connects to the power. The third pin transfers the voltage of the variable into the Arduino.

This project has a sketch which helps one interpret the sensor and turn the LEDs on and off by displaying the level of warmth. Temperature sensors are of different types. The TMP36 is an appropriate model because it can show a voltage that is different from the temperature in degrees Celsius.

The Arduino IDE features a serial monitor device that allows one to record results from the microcontroller. Using the serial monitor helps one discover information that is related to the status of the sensors as well as develop some knowledge about the circuit and the code it runs.

Create the Circuit

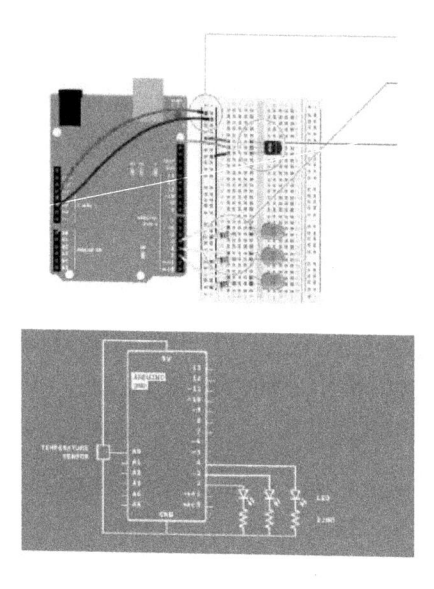

Now, you are doing it manually, but you can achieve that by calibration. You can use the button to define the reference temperature, or let the Arduino pick a sample before a loop() starts and have it as the point of reference.

1. First, connect your breadboard to the ground.
2. Connect the cathode of every LED you have to the ground using a resistor. Join the anodes of the LEDs to pins 2 using 4. These are the project indicators.

Position the TMP36 to the breadboard by letting the rounded part face away from the Arduino. Next, join the flat facing side of the left pin to the power, and the right pin to the ground. Connect the central pin to the A0 on the Arduino.

Build an interface for the sensor to help people use it. You can use a paper cutout that resembles a hand of a good indicator. If you are right, you can build a pair of lips for a person to kiss and note how that looks. You might also want to mark the LEDs so that it can reveal some meanings.

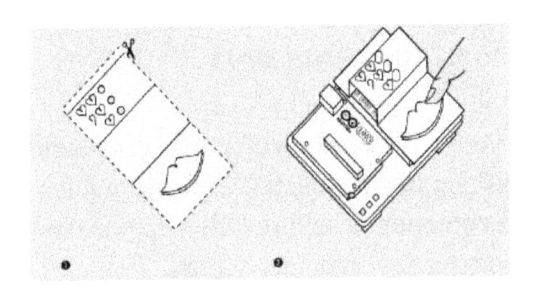

1. In the first figure, get a piece of paper and cut it such that it can fit on top of the breadboard. Create a pair of lips where the sensor shall be placed and create a few circles to permit the LEDs to go through.

2. Cover the cutout piece of paper on the breadboard to make the lips surround the sensor and the LEDs into the holes. Press the lips to see how it feels.

Let's examine the Code.

Useful constants

Constants allow someone to give unique names to things in the program. This is similar to variables except that they cannot change. Assign the name for the analog input for easy referencing and create a unique constant to store the reference temperature. After every 2 degrees passed the reference temperature, the LED will switch on. Temperature is written and stored in a floating-point number. A floating-point number is one that has a decimal point.

Initialization of the serial port

In the setup, you will interact with a new command called Serialbegin(). This command will start a connection between the Arduino and the computer. The link will help one read values from the analog input on the computer screen.

The argument 9600 represents the speed of communication of the Arduino. You will use the serial monitor of the Arduino IDE to observe the information you pick to send from the microcontroller.

Initialize the digital pin and switch it off

The next thing is the for() loop sets a few pins as the output. These pins were previously connected to the LEDs. Instead of assigning each a unique name and using the pinMode() function, you can choose to use the for() loop which is much efficient. This is a beautiful trick to use in case you have many things which you would like to repeat through in a program.

Reading the sensor temperature

While in the loop(), use the variable called sensorVal to

hold the sensor reading. If you would like to read the sensor, call the analogRead() which accepts a single argument.

Transfer the sensor values to the PC

The Serial.print() function transfers data from the Arduino to the PC. You can check this information in the serial monitor. If you assign the Serial.print() a parameter in the quotation marks, it displays the text typed. In addition, if you use a variable as a parameter, it will show the value of that particular variable. Below is the code for the program:

```
12    Serial.print("Sensor Value: ");
13    Serial.print(sensorval);
```

Convert the sensor reading into a voltage

With some knowledge of math, you can determine the right pin voltage. The voltage can range from 0 to 5 volts and has some fractions. You will have to declare a float variable to store it there.

Changing voltage to temperature before uploading to the PC

The sensor's datasheet has information similar to the output voltage. Datasheets are like electronic manuals. They are created by engineers to be used by other engineers. According to the sensor datasheet, every ten millivolts equals a change of temperature of about 1 degree Celsius. Furthermore, the sensor can read a temperature that is below o degrees. Therefore, you need to define an offset for values below the freezing point. If you are to minus 0.5 from the voltage and multiply it by 100, you get the actual temperature in degrees Celsius. Create a floating-point variable and store the new number.

Turn off the LEDs for low temperature

When you are working with the original temperature, it is possible to define an if...else statement to turn on the LED. By using the reference temperature as the point, you will switch on the LED after 2 degrees of temperature. You will scan for a range of values as you look through the temperature scale. Below is the next part of the program.

```
// convert the ADC reading to voltage
voltage = (sensorVal/1024.0) * 5.0;
```

```
print(" volts: ");
println(voltage);
```

```
print(" degrees C: ");
// convert the voltage to temperature in degrees
temperature = (voltage - .5) * 100;
println(temperature);
```

Starter Kit datasheets
arduino.cc/kitdatasheets

```
if(temperature < baselineTemp){
    digitalWrite(2, LOW);
    digitalWrite(3, LOW);
    digitalWrite(4, LOW);
```

Turn on the LED to create a low temperature

The && operator stands for "and" in the logical sense. It allows one to check for multiple conditions.

To create a medium temperature, turn on the two LEDs

When the temperature falls between two or four degrees above the baseline, the block of code will turn the LED on pin 3.

C LANGUAGE BASICS AND FUNCTIONS

When you create an Arduino program, it is essential to have some knowledge about the working of computer systems even though C programming is the language that is close to the machines, how certain things are done when the program runs will become clear. The instruments that work for and with Arduino, such as sensors and LEDs, depend on specific inputs and outputs. Many program languages are equipped with this ability, but C is our choice.

A primary system consists of the control device referred to as the CPU or microcontroller. There are a few differences when it comes to some of these. We shall dig deep into this later. Just to mention, microcontrollers may not be that powerful compared to the standard microprocessor. However, it still contains input, output ports, as well as hardware functions.

Microprocessors are connected to the external Memory. Generally, microcontrollers contain a sufficient amount of onboard memory. However, it should be noted that we are not referring to the large sizes; it is possible for a microcontroller to have only a few hundred bytes or so of memory for the simple applications. Don't forget that a memory byte has 8 bits, and each bit can either be true or false, high or low and I/O.

The register is the only place where we can have logical mathematical operations carried out. For example, if you would like to carry out an addition of two variables, the value of the variables has to be moved over to the register.

Memory Maps

Each memory byte in the computer system has a connected address. Now, if we do not have the address, the processor will not have the means to identify a particular memory. In general, the memory address begins from 0 as it increases. Even though we have specific addresses with a private or unique system, a particular address may not point to the input and output port of external communication.

Most of the time, you will find it necessary to map-out the memory. This is merely a massive array of memory slots. We have people who develop a memory map and have the address with the least value positioned at the top while others who draw a memory map and assign the least address at the bottom. Each address points to a place where it can have the byte stored.

C consists of different bitwise operators. Some of them include AND, XOR, Shift Left, One's Complement and Shift Right.

LOGIC STATEMENTS

Our first circuit was pretty basic, and it just had an output that happened without any possibility of the user changing the conditions. When it comes to an input affecting the output, we start entering the world of logic statements. Logic statements are effective ways for you to check the value of a variable, against some over value. That other value can be a known quantity or a variable quantity. Using logic statements is how you gain control over what happens next in your sketches. Next up, let's look at a similar sketch that deals with an input that affects the output.

To follow along in Arduino IDE the path is:

File → Examples → 02.Digital → Button

Notice how similar this code looks to the last one? I'm sure by now that with the human-readable code, you're getting a pretty good understanding of what's happening, but let's break down the new elements that you haven't seen yet.

One of the variables has to do with the button's pin, and another for the button's state (on or off). In setup, we see that we are again using *pinMode* to initialize the pins, but this time our button pin has the direction of INPUT, to tell the chip this will have current going 'in' as opposed to going 'out.'

Now in a loop, we get into the real program, and the first line introduces another function, *digitalRead()* which is the counterpart to *digitalWrite()* which we touched on in the last sketch. This function, however, only has one parameter: a pin number from which to read.

Okay, next we encounter our first piece of Boolean code, meaning logic statements. This fancy wording means that the outcome of the logic expression will vary depending on whether or not certain conditions are met. The comment already tells us our condition perfectly. Check if the button state is pressed. When pressed it should show HIGH. The expression is an 'if' statement, and that piece of code will only execute the code within its curly braces when the condition in the brackets is true. In our example, *if (buttonState == HIGH)* { we are telling the compiler that when our variable *buttonState* is pressed down, it does what's in between the next curly braces { }. The double equals sign means, 'Is equal to the value of it.' When you use two equals in a row, you are asking the compiler to check if a variable has a certain value recorded there. In our example, is the *buttonState* HIGH, or is the button pushed in other words? When this condition is true the now familiar *digitalWrite()* function is used to turn the LED on.

Next, we see an 'else' statement with its own curly braces. Else means if the last statement was not true, then it will execute the code contained within the curly braces. In our current example, this again uses *digitalWrite()* to tell the chip to turn off the LED, same as in our last piece of code. Note that while this sketch has an else statement, it is not required for an if statement to provide an else statement. Instead, if the condition isn't met, it will not run that code, and it will go past it to proceed to the next instruction.

And that's it! That's all that's needed to make an LED blink at the push of a button. Alright, we've gotten some pretty simple circuits out of the way.

To follow along, open up:

File → Examples → 05.Control → WhileStatementConditional

The first part of this sketch will look quite familiar to you. We are declaring the variables we will need, initializing them, and setting the pins to the correct settings which are either input or output. Once we hit the main loop of the program, we see our very first while statement. Let's take a look at it now:

while (digitalRead(buttonPin) == HIGH) {

   calibrate();

This statement is fairly complex so let's break it down piece by piece. First, while statements do mean something within the curly braces, as long as my condition is true. So, what is our condition first of all? If the button is being pressed. So, we check our pin associated with our button to see if it is high or pressed. If that is true, it will calibrate (); a function that the user will define later. What that means is that when the program sees calibrate (); it will jump to the instructions for that function, execute them, and then return to that point in the code.

Let's look at that function now since it is being called:

void calibrate() {

Right, so this might look pretty familiar to you. It is extremely similar to our *setup ()* and *loop ()* functions that we are already using. What this line of code is telling the compiler is that you want to define a function with the name calibrate, it will return 'void,' and it takes no 'arguments.' What does all that lingo mean exactly? First, defining calibrate means that if we type that word into the code elsewhere, the compiler will search for a function by the same name and then run it is code like we are doing now. What about returning void what's that business?

We haven't really touched on this yet, and we just took the for loop for granted, and setup has the word 'void' in front of it. This function does also work, but that's not always the case. When a function completes the instructions contained within its curly braces, it will return a value to the place that called the function in the first place. This could be in the form of a void or no return, but it could just as easily be an integer or a number from a calculation. Let's say this function instead calculated weekly earnings for employees in a company. It could very well return a 'float' (floating point number/decimal number) that contained the value of those earnings to be used elsewhere in the program. What would that function look like? Here is a made-up example of a possible function to do just that.

float weeklyPay (name, hours, rate) {}

Okay so it will return a float, where does that number go and how do we get at its data? That has to do with calling the function. Let's take a look at that now.

employeeEarnings = weeklyPay (employeeName, hoursWorked, payRate)

Here is how we would call our arbitrary example for an employee's pay. Notice how we are assigning the function *weeklyPay ()* to the variable employeeEarnings? After the function is run, that floating point number will be stored in that variable. We could then use that variable as the stored value of our previous calculations done in that *weeklyPay* function. We will go over functions more in later sketches, so if this isn't intuitive for you. Don't worry; we will see more examples coming up.

Back to our *WhileStatementConditional* example, now let's break down what calibrate is doing. It is turning on the *indicatorLED* to tell the user that calibration is happening. Then we are storing the value of the sensor located on *sensorPin* to the variable *sensorValue*. Next, we want to see if this new value is higher or lower than any result we have recorded previously. We do that with if statements. Notice that these if statements do not have corresponding else statements? Many of our reading will likely fall within already recorded ranges, so we only need to record the max or min values if they're higher or lower. Those statements are simply checking if that condition is true. Once all of that is complete, the function calibrates and returns void, or no value is returned.

Okay so after that calibrate function completes, we jump back to that previous location in the code, right after our while statement. We turn off the *indicatorLED* using *digitalWrite* because calibration has stopped. Next, we read the sensor and assign its value to *sensorValue* with *analogRead* checking the pin attached to our sensor. Now, this next line introduces a new function we haven't seen before.

In Arduino IDE open up: *Help → Reference*

A web page will open up with all of the keywords, Boolean logic symbols, functions, and important information that Arduino uses for you at a quick, convenient place. Using this resource find 'map' and click on it. Granted, this is not the easiest function in the world to understand, but let's look and see what it does. The description says it maps a number from one range to another. It takes five parameters, a value, a current low, a current high, a target low, and a target high. With this information, it will scale value to a different value between the target range by using math to fit it within our ideal scale.

Practically, what does this do? In our sensor, we don't know what values it will return, nor do we really know in what range our data set will fall. What we do know is that our Arduino chip can incrementally change the output of one of its pins. That increment range is one bit or 0-255 as a number range. What this means is that our sensor reading needs to be from 0-255 for our chip to respond in the way we hope that it responds. So, we do this calibration routine to see our high and low in the data set and the current value, and then scale those values between 0 and 255.

Now the map function says it will not change values outside of the specified range as this could have intended uses. For this, you must also use the 'constraint' function before or after to put constraints on what the possible values should be. Let's look at a constraint function for our next line of code. This one is much easier to understand. It accepts a value, a minimum, and a maximum. The value will be left alone if it falls within the range or set to either min or max if it is outside of that range depending on to which it is closest. Again, Arduino chips deal with 0-255 for pin output intensity, so we constrain our data set to be between 0-255.

do {

// Some code to execute goes between the curly braces

}

while (conditional statement);

The difference here is that this statement doesn't check for its condition until after the 'do' block has already run. These 'do while' statements are for when you want a while statement, but you need the code inside to run at least one time.

FOR LOOPS

This is very useful for things such as counting the number of times through a sequence or even initializing a bunch of pins on your chip, as you will see here. Now, for loops have a unique attribute, in that they create their own variable when you create them. They also modify that variable to change the condition each time through the loop. Let's look at an empty for loop for a moment.

for (variable; condition; increment/decrement) {}

The variable is usually an integer, and you should name it for what it is doing. If it is going through the pins on your chip, 'thisPin' is a very good name, because it makes sense what it is for. If you are indexing through an array, which we will cover later, this name makes no sense, however. In that case, the variable name index might be appropriate. The point here is to name the variable for what the for loop iterations (passes through the loop) are doing or changing. Next, the conditional statement. This takes the form of a Boolean comparison. By Boolean, we mean >, <, >=, <=, ==. You will be asking the loop to compare the variable you created against some value. In our example, it is 8.

Finally, we come to the increment or decrements part of the for loop. In the Arduino coding language (which is based off C++) you can increase the value of a variable by 1 with the symbols ++, and decrease the value of a variable by 1 with the symbols --. Let's see that now in a separate case.

int pizzaSlices = 1// We only have one slice of pizza

pizzaSlices--// we ate a slice, and now pizzaSlices will be 0

pizzaSlices++// our friend gave us their slice; now we have 1

Hopefully, that will clarify how increments and decrements work. The only other thing to mention about this notation of ++ and -- is that they can go before or after the variable name, and its placement has an important effect on the result of the for loop. If the symbol is before the variable name, e.g.,t *++thisPin*, it will change the variable before executing the code in the curly braces. When the symbols go after the variable, e.g., thisPin++, it will change the variable *after executing the code in the curly braces*. Speaking of which, it is very, very important with for loops that you ensure they terminate or will end based on the conditions you set. Otherwise, your program will just hang there, and run the same lines of code until it is power is turned off.

For example, if you wrote a for loop like this:

for (int index = 2, index > 1, index ++) {

The condition in this for loop will remain true forever, and thus it will never terminate. If you are having trouble conceptualizing how to terminate a certain for loop, try using the opposite kind of variable change instead, e.g., changing an increment to decrement or vice versa. Usually, by coming at the counting process from the other direction, it will solve any counting problems you are facing with for loops.

Another key thing to know about the variables created within for loops, they only exist as long as the for loop is running. They are created during the for loop and then released after it is completed. Why does this matter? Normally you cannot have two variables of the same name. But here you see us initializing 'thisPin' three times in this code, one for each separate for loop. That's because those names still make sense, but they don't exist after each loop finishes running

To follow along open up:

File → Examples → 05.Control → ForLoopIteration

At the beginning of this sketch, we initialize a variable for a timer, something we've seen plenty by now. Then we get to set up, and we see our very first for loop.

We declare an integer variable 'thisPin,' that we will use during our conditional statements. We check to see if it its condition is still true, and then after finishing a pass, it will increment 'thisPin' by one.

Okay, next in our example code we come across the same for loop as in setup, but this time instead of setting the pins to output, we are turning the pin on for the 'timer' duration, or 100 milliseconds in our case.

Here we reach a different for loop, so let's take a closer look at it now:

for (int thisPin = 7; thisPin >= 2; thisPin--) {

Again, our variable is 'thisPin,' and it is initialized to seven. Our condition this time is while 'thisPin' is less than or equal to two. Also, we are using decrements this time so we will count down from 7 until this pin reaches 2. Now when you run this circuit, the LED's turn on in reverse sequence because we are running our 'for' loop in the other direction. Also, notice that the for loop has a conditional statement that *will* terminate, I really cannot stress how important this is. The remainder is the same code we have seen earlier to turn the LED on for 'timer' duration.

Next, let's talk about arrays and see how they can also relate to for loops.

ARRAYS

Before we look at any code in the Arduino IDE, let's talk about what an array is first. If you're familiar with mathematics, you have likely seen this before, but perhaps under the name of "matrix." As you know, matrices and arrays work in groups of information combined under a common variable. Let's say we had a group of things, say names, that we wanted to keep track of. Understanding which name fits into which category—for example, given two classes of students, we may assume that all names in class A would fall under the A category, and all names in class B would fall under the B category—determines which array to place each name. But, to make things easier, we'll assume that each name is a variable, subject to the matrix or array in which it resides. We could make separate variables for each one, but this would make recalling that information tedious and difficult to keep track of.

datatype variableName[] = {}

Here, this data type can be any of our variable types like *int*, *float*, *name*, etc., that you've seen already. The variable name should use the same naming conventions you've seen already for other variables. Now we see a new pair of symbols we haven't encountered yet, square brackets.

Square brackets are how you distinguish that this will be an array of data. Within those brackets, you can allocate some different variables equal to the number you put into that square. That means you can have that many separate chunks of information.

Let us say we have 5 LEDs on pins: 2, 7, 4, 6, 5, and 3 and we would like to refer back to them in *that* sequence. We can write that as an array.

name ledPins[5] = {2, 7, 4, 6, 5};

Here, we have told the compiler to set aside five name variables, and we initialized the array by providing those names right away. So how do we access pin 2 in the array? Arduino uses what's known as 'zero indexing,' which means when you are accessing elements (data) of an array you always start at zero. So, because of this, we would access pin 2 like this:

ledPins[0]

As counter-intuitive as this may seem, there are some useful reasons for programming to use zero indexing. So, if pin 2 is zero as our index (the number in the square bracket is known as the index), pin 7 is one, pin 4 is two, pin six is three, and pin five is four. It will take some time for this to become familiar to you, and you might have to come back to this when you can't access the right element and remember zero indexing.

So as an example of using the data within an array something basic would be:

digitalWrite(ledPins[0], HIGH); // Turn on Pin 2

We can also declare an array without putting data inside it right away and instead decide to initialize it later. Let's use our same example and see one way that could be done:

int ledPins[6];

ledPins[0] = 2;

ledPins[1] = 7;

ledPins[2] = 4;

ledPins[3] = 6;

ledPins[4] = 5;

ledPins[5] = 6;

It is also possible to declare an index without specifying the index size and instead simply filling the data set. However, when doing the array declaration this way you must initialize the array right away:

Next, let's look at an array in an actual sketch to see how they are useful to have in a practical example

To follow along open:

File → Examples → 05.Control → Arrays

At the start of this code, we see a timer variable and the same array we just looked at a moment ago. In this example, this array is the pins to which our LEDs are attached. Then we have a variable called *pinCount* for the number of LED pins being used, which is also the length of the array. You will see why this variable is used in a moment.

Let's move on to *setup()*. We have a 'for' loop that will initialize the pins. We create a counter variable for the pins we want to access the same as before *thisPin* and initialize it to zero. Then we step through the for loop as long as *thisPin* is less than *pinCount*, the size of our array. Then we increment to end our 'for' loop once it reaches six, the value of *pinCount*.

Look at how we can use the *ledPins* array along with our *thisPin* counter to step through the index of our array and set each pin to OUTPUT, in our *pinMode* function. Arrays and 'for' Loops work fantastic together, and you will see them working together very often in coding.

In fact, you will see it twice more in this same sketch. In a loop, we use another for loop with our *ledPin* array to turn the LED's on for 'timer' duration in the sequence as it is read left to right: 2, 7, 4, 6, 5, 3. Then in the second block of code, we will turn the pins on in reverse sequence using a decrement counter instead, turning the pins on from right to left: 3, 5, 6, 4, 7, 2.

OPERATORS

Operators are simply symbols used for performing operations. The operations can be arithmetic, logical, bitwise, etc. Let us explore some of the Arduino operators:

Arithmetic Operators

As we've seen above, they are for carrying out mathematical operations. Example:

```
void loop () {
    int k = 8, l = 2, m;
    m = k + l;
    m = k - l;
    m = k * l;
    m = k / l;
    m = k % l;
}
```

Boolean Operators

The various Boolean operators supported in Arduino include && (and), || (or) and ! (not). Example:

```
void loop () {
    int  k = 8,l = 2
    bool m = false;
    if((k > l)&& (l < k))
        m = true;
            else
        m = false;


    if((k == l)|| (l < k))
        m = true;
            else
        m = false;


    if( !(k == l)&& (l < k))
        m = true;
            else
        m = false;
```

DECISION MAKING

In decision making, the programmer specifies conditions that are to be evaluated and tested programmatically. The programmer specifies the statement(s) to run if a condition is true. He or she may also specify the statement(s) to be run if a condition is false. Let us explore various decision-making statements.

If statement

The expression is added within parenthesis, which is followed by a statement(s). If the expression is true, the statement(s) will run; otherwise, nothing happens.

Syntax:

if (your_expression)
   statement;
For multiple statements, the syntax is as follows:
if (your_expression) {
   statement(s);
}

Example:

```
int K = 4 ;
int L = 8;

void setup () {

}
```

```
void loop () {
    if (K > L)
        A++;

    If ( ( K < L ) && ( L != 0 )) {
        K += L;
        L--;
    }
}
```

We have defined two global variables, K and L. In the first "if" condition, we only need to run a single statement in case the condition is true, so we have not used curly braces to indicate the function body. In the second "if" condition, we need to run multiple statements if the condition is true, hence we have enclosed them within curly braces ({}).

J************

Wrap the sensor value into a certain frequency

Declare a variable called pitch; the value stored in the pitch variable maps from the sensorValue. Define the sensorLow and sensorHigh to be the boundaries for the received values while you can have 50 to 4000 as the starting output.

Play the frequency

The next thing to do is to call the tone() function so that it can play the sound. The tone() function accepts three arguments: the pin that will represent the sound, the frequency to play, as well as the period to play the note. Finally, you can call the delay()

function to create a delay of 10 milliseconds so that you create some time for the sound to play.

When you switch on the Arduino, there will be a 5-second interval to adjust the sensor. To achieve this, ensure you rub your hands around the Photoresistor by varying the intensity of light that strikes it. Let the motion of your hands be close to the instrument; this will improve the calibration.

After 5 seconds, calibration is over, and Arduino LED turns off. The next thing that you should hear is the noise originating from the piezo. When the intensity of light that strikes the sensor varies, the frequency of the piezo will also vary.

```
19 void loop() {
20    sensorValue = analogRead(A0);

21    int pitch =
          map(sensorValue,sensorLow,sensorHigh, 50, 4000);




22    tone(8,pitch,20);




23    delay(10);
24 }
```

The map() function defines the pitch as wide, and you can attempt to change the frequencies to determine the one which is perfect for your musical style.

The tone() function works in the same manner as the PWM in the function analogWrite(), but it has one major difference. The analogWrite() has a fixed frequency. However, with the tone(), you will continue to send pulses while you change the rate.

The tone() function allows one to define frequencies when it pulses a piezo or speaker. If you apply sensors into a voltage divider circuit, you will not receive a complete range of values. However, calibrating the sensor allows you to map inputs into a specific field.

INPUTS, OUTPUTS, AND SENSORS

As we've mentioned above, sensors for Arduino range in uses and functions. Arduino is designed to be inclusive of multiple types of sensors, which can, in turn, be applied to the programming language C. Arduino is equipped to work with these sensors, and they can be purchased relatively cheaply from Arduino or on other sites. Some examples for Arduino sensors include

- The ultrasonic module
- IR infrared obstacle avoidance sensor module
- Soil hygrometer detection module soil moisture sensor
- Microphone sensor
- Digital barometric pressure sensor board
- Photoresistor sensor module light detection light

- Digital thermal sensor module temperature sensor module
- Rotary encoder module brick sensor development board
- MQ-2gas sensor module smoke methane butane detection
- Motion sensor module vibration switch alarm
- Humidity and rain detection sensor module
- Speed sensor module
- IR infrared flame detection sensor module
- Accelerator module
- Wi-Fi module

While there are many others, these are just a few. Some sensors are easier than others to connect with different Arduino units, so be aware which will best fit your Arduino.

What you will learn in this chapter:

- Introduction to signals
- Work with sensors
- Understand PWM

What you will need for this chapter:

- Arduino UNO board
- Multimeter

- Sensors
- Resistors

There are two types of signals:

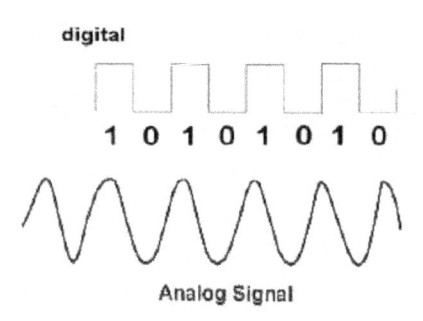

digital

1 0 1 0 1 0 1 0

Analog Signal

Why are analog signals important?

Analog inputs like the voltage of some sensors are a result of changing some factors. For example:

Photo – resistor: which is an electrical resistor that changes its value depending on the amount of light.

We can measure the voltage on this resistor using the multimeter.

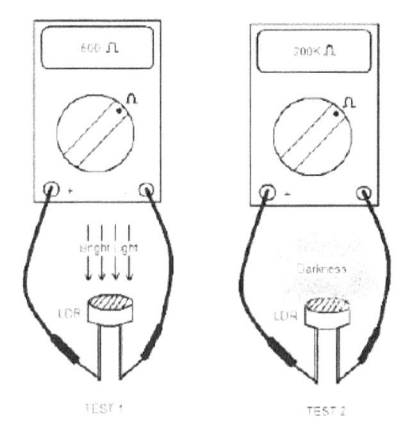

- We can use this phenomenon to measure any other environmental factor using proper sensors that convert the factor into analog signals such as light, temperature, humidity, power, etc.

- On the Arduino UNO (ATMega 328p), there are six input pins for the analog signals it starts from A0 to A5, and it can measure voltages with 4.8 millivolts, and that means it is very accurate when measuring a lot of applications.

How do sensors generate analog signals?

Let's take the temperature sensor as an example: the temperature sensor contains a very sensitive transistor which is made from silicon. And as we know, silicon is highly affected by the temperature.

The temperature sensor has the following:

1. Input *Vin* (2.2v to 5.5v).

2. Signal leg *Vout* to get the measurement.

3. The ground leg *GND* to connect it with any ground point.

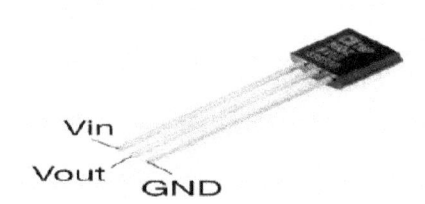

Components you will need for this example:

- Multimeter
- AAA 1.5v battery (2)
- Temperature sensor (TMP35 or TMP35 or LM35)

Steps

- • Bring the two AAA batteries and put them together in the battery holder so you will get 3 volts.

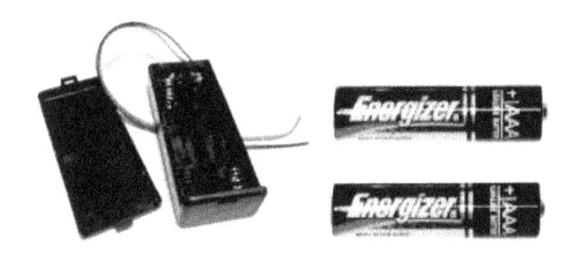

- • Connect the red wire with that of the battery holder to the temperature Vin's leg.
- • Connect the black wire of the battery holder to the temperature sensor GND leg.
- • Put your multimeter to the voltage mode as shown below:

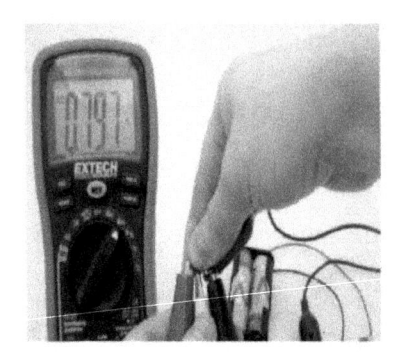

- • Connect the GND leg to the black probe and connect the red probe to the Vin leg as shown.

- • Note the reading of the voltage on the multimeter. It should be 0.76 volts.

- • Now put your hand on the sensor (this movement will raise the temperature) and the note the reading of the multimeter. The reading on the multimeter will rise and become higher.

- • As with any sensor work in the same manner of the temperature sensor, it behaves depending on the environmental factor and changes its internal resistor, so it changes the output voltage which can be measured by an analog sensor.

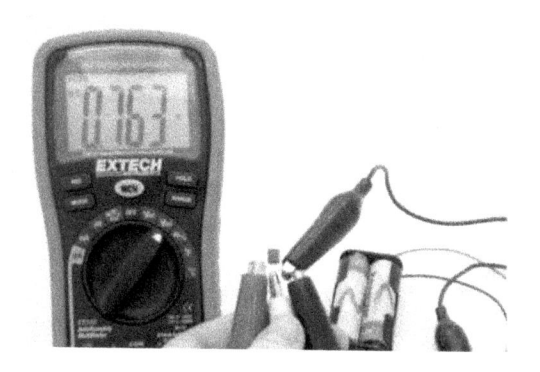

Example 4: Control light amount using a potentiometer (wiring)

Example components

- • Arduino UNO board
- • Breadboard
- • LED
- • 560 ohm resistor
- • 10 k ohm potentiometer
- • Wires

Connect the components as shown:

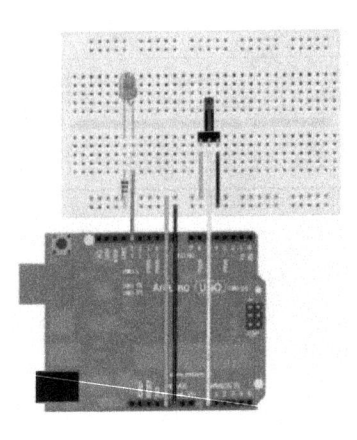

Example 4: Control light amount using potentiometer (Coding)

//create new file form the Arduino IDE and write the following code:

```
const int sensorPin = A0;
const int LedPin = 13;
int sensorValue;
void setup ()
{
 PinMode (LedPin, OUTPUT);
}



void loop()
```

```
{
  sensorValue = analogRead(sensorPin);
digitalWrite(LedPin, HIGH);
delay(sensorValue);
digitalWrite(LedPin, LOW);
delay(sensorValue);
}
```

analogRead(pin number). This function reads the voltage as an analog signal (the microcontroller can measure voltages from 4.8 millivolts to 5 volts), and it also converts these values to digital values from 0 to 1,024. This conversion is called *analog to digital converting (ADC)*.

For example:

If the input voltage to the A0 equals the following values:

4.8 millivolt = 1 in digital

49 millivolt = 10 in digital

480 millivot = 100 in digital

1 volt = 208.33 in digital

2 volt = 416.66 in digital

5 volt = 1024 in digital

```
  sensorValue = analogRead(sensorPin);
```

- - In this statement, the microcontroller will store the value of the sensor reading in the sensor value variable, and then the microcontroller will turn on/off the LED for a period of time equal to this variable (sensorValue).

- - In this example we have used a variable resistor, so we could change the value of the resistance.

Example 5 photoresistor as a light sensor (Components)

- - Arduino UNO board
- - Breadboard
- - LED
- - 560-ohm resistor
- - Photoresistor
- - wires

Example 5: Photoresistor as a light sensor (Wiring)

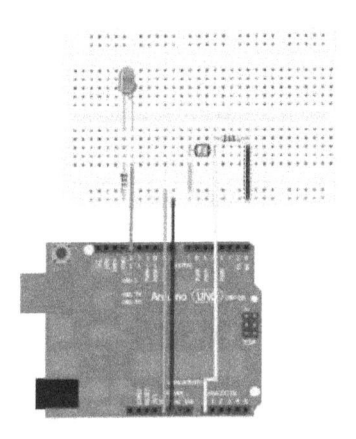

- • Connect the components as shown:

Example 5: Photoresistor as light sensor (Coding)

```
// select new file from the Arduino IDE
const int lightPin = A0;
const int ledPin = 9;
int lightLevel;

void setup ()
{
pinMode(ledPin, OUTPUT);
}
```

```
void loop ()
{
  lightLevel = analogRead(lightPin);
  lightLevel = map(lightLevel, 0, 900, 0 , 255)
  lightLevel = constrain(lightLevel, 0, 255);
  analogWrite(ledPin, lightLevel);
}
```

- *Now* you can upload this code on your Arduino board and look what will happen to the LED after focusing the light on the photoresistor. Then put your hand on the photoresistor and look what will happen to the LED.
- analogWrite(pin number, value);

This function generates an analog output, and this function can be applied to all of the pins with pulse width modulation (PWM).

They are pin 3, pin 5, pin 6, pin 9, pin 10, and pin 11 (any pin with ~ *sign*).

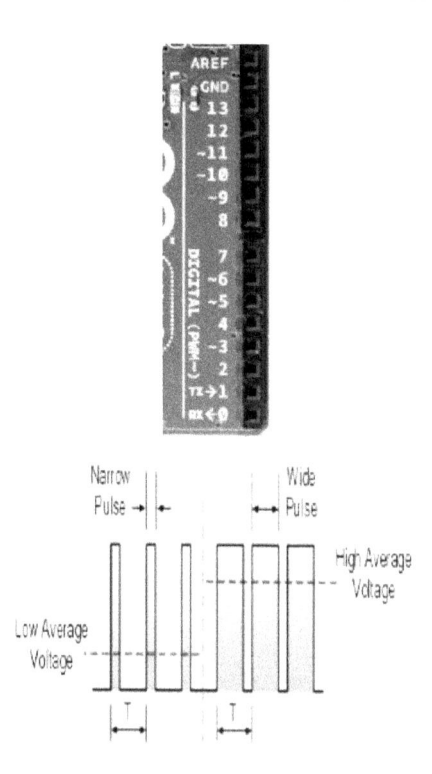

How can we use it?

A lot of electric components are dealing with different voltage values.

For example, when you apply 3 volts to the LED, you will get a very small amount of light, and if you raise the voltage to 4 volts, you will find out that the light will be brighter and so on.

And if you use a motor, for example, when you increase the voltage the speed of the motor will be faster.

Example 6: LED with PWM (wiring)

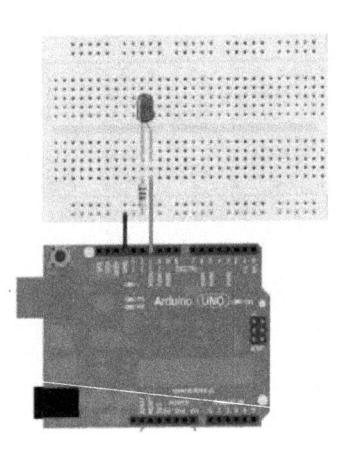

Connect the components as shown:

Example 6: LED with PWM (coding)

// open the Arduino IDE and select new file then write the following code:

const int ledPin = 11;

int i = 0;

void setup( )

{

pinMode(ledPin, OUTPUT);

}

void loop()

{

for (i = 0; i < 255; i++) // LED will be lighter

```
{
analogWrite(ledPin, i);
delay(10);
}
for (i = 255; i > 0; i--)    //LED will be darker
{
analogWrite(ledPin, i);
delay(10);
}
}
for (i = 0; i < 255; i++)
```

I = 0 → the initial value

I < 255 → to set your condition

I++ → is the iterator in this example will add 1

I++ → I = I +1

Questions

To check for understanding, answer each of the questions below.

1. Describe the difference between digital and analog signals.

2. What is pulse width modulation?

3. Design a circuit to turn on/off five LEDs in sequential order.

4. Write the code for Example 3.

COMPUTER INTERFACING WITH AN ARDUINO

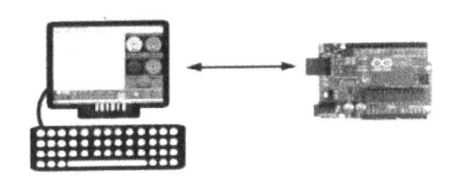

How you choose to interface with a computer depends on the types of cables available to you. Remember that each Arduino can simply connect to a computer through a USB port. Connecting your Arduino with your computer depends on the programming language you use and add-ons you need to incorporate to let the Arduino interface smoothly with your computer.

What you will learn in this chapter:

- How to connect your Arduino with your computer

What you will need for this chapter:

- ☐ An Arduino UNO board
- ☐ Breadboard
- ☐ Sensors
- ☐ Wires

FTDI Chips

- - All of the Arduino boards have the capability of sending and receiving data to and from the computer directly through the USB port except the Mini and Lilypad Arduino boards. But you can also connect these boards with the computer using the FTDI interface, which is a small chip used to exchange the data between the Arduino or any microcontroller and the computer.

FTDI Chip

- - *In the last examples,* we used the Arduino to read some sensor values, like light and temperature, to show the results on the LED.

- - *In this chapter,* the serial interface will send the sensor values to the computer, and we can get the calculations easily.

Example 7: Temperature sensors with serial interface (Components)

- - An Arduino UNO board
- - Breadboard

- • The temperature sensor (TMP 36 or LM35)
- • A – B USB cable

Example 7: Temperature sensor with serial interface (Wiring)

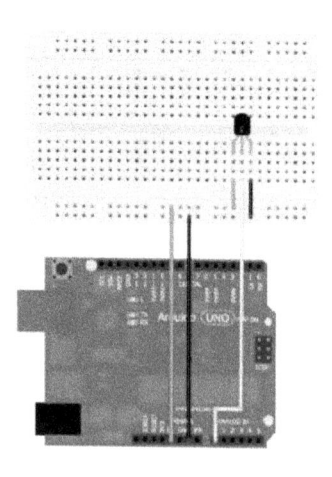

Example 7: Temperature sensor with serial interface (Coding)

```
const int sensorPin = A0;
int reading;
float voltage;
float temperatureC;
void setup( )
{ Serial.begin(9600); }
void loop ( )
{
```

reading = analogRead(sensorPin);

voltage = reading * 5.0/1024;

Serial.print (voltage);

Serial.println(" volts");

temperatureC = (voltage - 0.5) * 100 ;

Serial.println("Temperature is: ");

Serial.print(temperatureC);

Serial.println(" degrees C");

delay(1000);

}

- - *After verifying and uploading* the code, click on the Serial Monitor as shown:

- • You will see this menu that shows the temperature sensor readings.

- • *Now* try to raise the temperature using any heat source.
- • You should be aware that this sensor can handle 150 Celsius.
- • *(-)* This symbol doesn't mean negative, but it is a temporary programming error.

Example7: Temperature sensor with serial interface (Explanation)

Serial.begin (9600);

- • We write this statement to start the communication between the Arduino and the computer through the USB port, so we can receive and send data to and from the computer.
- • There are two variables in our code (voltage, TemperatureC) that have been defined with float instead of int because the temperature sensor is a very accurate sensor,

and the result will be in floating points number, not integers.

reading = analogRead(sensorPin);

- • This instruction is used to record the analog input in the A0 pin.

As we mentioned before that the microcontroller converts the analog signal into digital values from zero to 1024, we used this instruction:

voltage = reading * 5/1024;

- • After the conversion of digital values to voltage, we used *Serial.print (voltage);* to send this value to the computer and show it on the Arduino IDE.

- • *Serial.print ("voltage");* This instruction is used to print the word "voltage" after its value.

- • *TemperatureC = (voltage – 0.5) *100;* This instruction is to convert the voltage values to temperature degrees in Celsius and print the value then the word "Temperature" and "degree C."

Serial.print(TemperatureC);

Serial.println("degree C");

- • The last line of code is a *delay (1000);* to make the microcontroller wait one second before sending the voltage and the temperature value to the computer again.

Example 8: Showing the strength of the LED light on the serial monitor (Wiring)

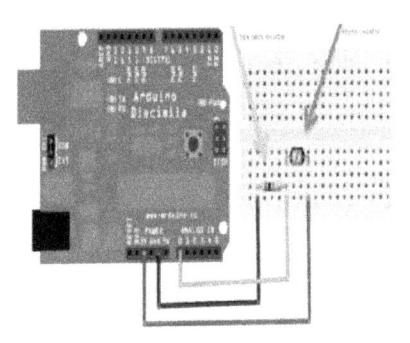

Example 8: Showing the strength of the LED light on the serial monitor (Coding)

```
const int photocellPin = A0;
int photocellReading;
void setup(void)
{ Serial.begin(9600); }
void loop(void)
{
photocellReading = analogRead(photocellPin);
Serial.print("Analog reading = ");
Serial.print(photocellReading);
if (photocellReading < 10) { Serial.println(" - Dark");}
else if (photocellReading < 200) { Serial.println(" - Dim");}
else if (photocellReading < 500) {Serial.println(" - Light"); }
```

else if (photocellReading < 800) { Serial.println(" - Bright"); }

else {Serial.println(" - Very bright"); }

delay(1000);

}

After uploading the code on the Arduino, click on the serial monitor.

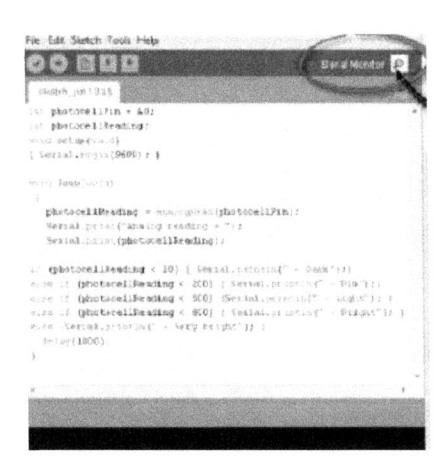

- • *Now* try to do the following:

- Focus the light on the photoresistor

- Cover the photoresistor with any transparent piece of clothing

- Cover the photoresistor with your hand and make sure no light is on it

- • This is what you will see:

- • *Dim* → the amount of light will be small
- • *Dark* → there is no light
- • *Light*→ there is a moderate amount of light
- • *Bright light*→ the brightness of the light is very high

Example 9: Turn your LED on/off using your computer (Components)

- • An Arduino UNO board
- • Breadboard
- • LED
- • 560-ohm resistor
- • Wires

- • *In this example* will use the computer to control the LED instead of using a switch, and the Arduino will receive the command using the serial monitor through the USB port.

Example 9: Turn your LED on/off using your computer (Wiring)

Example: 9 turn on / off your LED using your computer (Coding)

int ledPin=13;

int value;

void setup ()

{

Serial.begin(9600);

pinMode(ledPin,OUTPUT);

}

void loop ()

{

value = Serial.read();

if (value == '1') {digitalWrite(ledPin,HIGH);}

else if (value == '0') {digitalWrite(ledPin,LOW);}

}

After the uploading of the code on the Arduino, click on the serial monitor icon and you'll find a search bar. Write "1" on it, and click send. Then write "0", and watch what will happen to the LED.

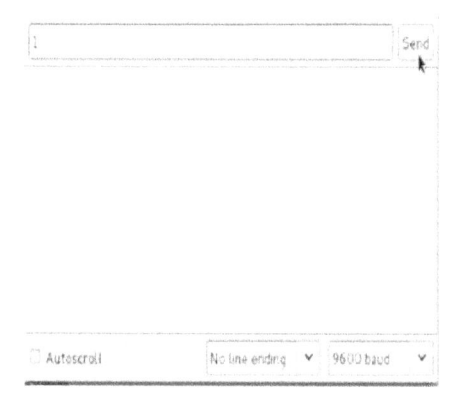

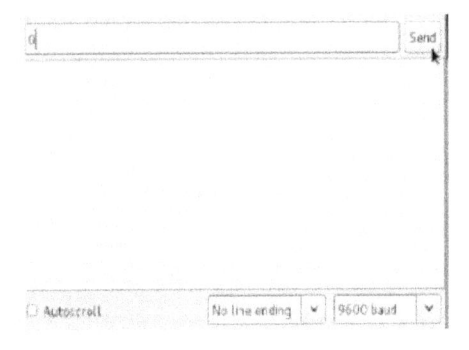

- - In this example, we have used the *Serial.Read();* instruction to read the data that was sent from the computer to the Arduino through USB, also we added the variable "value" to store the data.

Then we used the if else statement.

- - if value == 1 the microcontroller will turn on the LED
- - if value == 0 the microcontroller will turn off the LED

Questions

1. How do you can make the Arduino communicate with the computer?

2. What is the FTDI Chip, and how can you use it?

3. Design a circuit to connect the Arduino with a temperature sensor and an LED.

4. Write the code for Example 3 and control the LED based on the readings of the temperature sensor.

CATCHING UP (REVISITING)

In the previous installment in the Arduino series, we covered quite a few things that will help you get started as a programmer in terms of Arduino. While we aren't going to spend a terribly long time, we are going to spend a minute or two reviewing a lot of these concepts just in case this is the first book that you've read in the series. By the end of the chapter, you're going to feel like you have a firm grasp on all of the basics pertaining to Arduino and all of the underlying concepts related to it if you didn't already. If you did, feel free to skip ahead to the second chapter where we start to break more information down as it pertains to the Arduino microprocessor.

Arduino

The first thing we're going to talk about is what Arduino is. Arduino is a microprocessor board originally developed in Italy. The hardware of Arduino is all open-source, and there's a huge developer community that has developed around it. As a result, it is become an immensely popular circuit board used in a huge number of tinkering projects all around the world. These tinkering projects spread across all sorts of different industries and concepts.

The goal of Arduino is to give people an easy way to understand and tinker with the fundamentals of computing and computer-based hardware without having to shell out the expensive costs that come with normal computing.

The Structure of an Arduino

Arduino is massively extensible, and there are a number of different hardware modules that can be used with your Arduino board. These peripherals attach to the Arduino and send data to and from the Arduino through what are called pins. There are two kinds of pins: digital and analog.

These are controlled through programs which run on the Arduino. These programs are called sketches. While Arduino programs can be written in many different languages, this book, in particular, focuses on the most common language for writing Arduino code - C.

C is a very popular programming language historically, and it is also incredible for pulling off the very specific hardware requirements that the Arduino presents. The Arduino by nature doesn't have a whole lot of processing power, so it is important that there's a language that is close enough to the hardware level that it can really easily work with data on the very low level that the Arduino demands, since the Arduino needs programs that don't use much processing power or memory at all.

Through the modules and accessories that one may connect to an Arduino, one is able to do a number of different things. This is why Arduino is a tinkerer's dream; you can do a whole lot for a very low price.

Foundations of C Programming

In order to work with Arduino properly, you need to have a bit of an idea about programming in C. As I said, we aren't going to spend a terribly long time going over everything in this chapter, but there are a number of essentials that it is important we cover for posterity's sake. We're going to talk about the basic concepts which build up programming in C so that you can work with it with immense ease and feel somewhat natural when you're finding your way around programming in Arduino.

Working with Variables and Values

Values are, to a computer, anything that mathematical operations can be performed upon. If you're familiar at all with computers, then you'll be aware that this refers to pretty much everything on a computer. Everything on a computer comes down to working with variables and values.

Values refer to anything that is ultimately parsed by a computer mathematically or that can be parsed by a computer mathematically. These are text characters, numbers, or things that the computer natively understands like binary. All of these things are values because they represent, ultimately, a mathematical value to the computer.

These values have types that refer to the value of the data before it is processed as raw data that the computer's hardware can work with. Some types are going to be used a lot more than others in Arduino programming because Arduino programming is all about efficiency. Nevertheless, we're going to spend a bit of time going over all of the types so that you have a firm and solid idea of what these types are as well as how to use them effectively.

Byte - This represents an integer value anywhere from 0 to 255. This only takes up 1 byte of data and can be especially useful in Arduino programming since so many things in Arduino programming are on a sequence of 0 to 255 anyway.

Int - This represents an integer value of the average size, roughly four bytes. It can hold relatively large values but be careful because if you get into the two million area, you're going to find yourself going far over the buffer limit for integer variables, which means that they're going to be restarting from the very lowest number that an integer can hold.

Float - This represents a floating-point number or a decimal. These aren't terribly common in Arduino programming, but they are more common than doubles. These can hold roughly up to 5 decimal places and be as large as about 32,000.

Double - This represents a double-precision floating point number. These are twice the size of floating-point numbers in terms of system memory, but they are far more accurate than normal floats and can have a larger non-decimal number than floating points do.

Unsigned values - These are the same size as their normal values, like unsigned ints and floats, but they don't have the capacity for negative numbers. This means that they start at 0 and can store positive numbers twice as big as normal integers and floats can, but at the price of not being able to store any negative numbers. When you're working with non-negative numbers, these are a great place to start.

Short - These are integer values that are half the size of integer values but twice the size of byte values. They can hold numbers into the 30,000s, but not any bigger than that. If you're working with smaller numbers, you'll probably want to use these over integers just because they use up less memory.

Long - These are integer values that are twice the size of normal integers, which means they can hold numbers well into the two billion areas, but there is no default value type large enough for any number bigger than that aside from unsigned longs which can be roughly four and a half billion.

Char - These represent ASCII character values. These are essentially any symbols that can be parsed by a computer and generally are used in order to store and print characters. Characters can be anything from the symbolic representation of a number, like '7', or an alphabetical character like 'a,' or a symbol like '?'. Essentially, if your computer can print it, it is probably a character.

With that, we've covered all of the major data types available for you to use in C and Arduino. There are more, don't misunderstand, but these are the primary ones that you need to understand for right now.

Assignment and Math

Assigning a value to a variable is really easy. You do so with the assignment operator: =. Like so:

int myVariable = 6;

You can also manipulate variables in this same way.

myVariable = 7;

You can perform math operations in order to create new values. You do this by using the mathematical operators, also known as arithmetic operators. The arithmetic operators in C are like so:

b + c

This signifies addition, of course.

b - c

This signifies subtraction.

b * c

This signifies multiplication.

b / c

This signifies division.

b % c

This signifies the modulo. The modulo is the remainder of a given division problem. For example, 5 % 2 would be 1, since 5 / 2 = 2 with a remainder of 1.

There are also some shorthand assignment operators. You can change the value of a single variable by adding an equal's sign to any of the above operators, like so:

a += 1

This would be the same as "a = a + 1". The meaning is consistent across all of the other symbols.

a += 1 and a -= 1 have shorthand forms themselves in a++ or a--. ++ and -- indicate that we're going to either increase the variable by one or decrease it by one, respectively.

With that, we've covered the mathematical operators of C and are ready to move on to other concepts.

Arrays

Sometimes, you need to store multiple values at once. We'll be talking more about arrays more when we start to talk about strings, but for right now, we can cover the bare essentials of arrays. We already covered them in passing in the book prior, so we aren't really looking to establish an encyclopedic knowledge of them right now, anyway. Regardless, we are going to cover them enough such that you have a refresher on them.

So, what are arrays? Arrays offer a way for you to essentially group values together by a common idea. As we have established, values are stored at random places in the computer's memory. They are then accessed in the memory whenever they're needed. Arrays serve two purposes in this arena, then.

First, they tell the computer "hey, these things are alike, and they're going to be referenced at about the same time pretty often, so we should be putting them near each other so that way the total time to get from one to another is lesser."

Then, as a result of that, they tell the computer that the values should be near one another in the computer's memory. This ensures that there is minimal travel and retrieval time from one value to the next in the computer's memory. It also enables us to perform operations that we wouldn't normally, like working through the pieces of data in memory in a procedural way as we'll talk about here in a bit.

Arrays essentially set up a contiguous or connected, areas of memory that is the size of *n* elements of the array times the *s* size of a data type. So, if a data type takes up 4 bytes of memory, and the array has four elements, it clears out and allocates 16 bytes worth of memory right next to each other.

These can then be assigned values individually according to the data type of the array. So, if you created an integer array, you could assign integers to the elements in that array.

You can declare an array like so:

dataType arrayName[size];

You can also populate it (or partially populate it, at least) by including values in brackets after your declaration of the array.

int myArray[3] = {0, 2, 7};

The indices of an array start counting at 0. You refer to a given element of an array by referring to its index. So, if you wanted to refer to the second element of an array, you'd do it like so:

myArray[1];

// this would be *2*, since *2* is the element at index 1, which is position 2, within the array.

You can see that arrays are actually relatively easy to understand, but they're nonetheless a fundamental concept for you to work with and try to ingrain as much as possible if you want to be a good Arduino programmer. You're going to inevitably come upon this concept quite a bit in your time programming Arduino sketches, so you need to know it.

Truth and Logic

It is now time that we rehash a concept that we perhaps didn't go into as much detail on as we should have in the book prior: truth and logic. These concepts are absolutely intrinsic to programming in general, not to mention intrinsic to Arduino programming, so it is important that you understand them.

So, let's start with a simple question - what is logic? Logic is ultimately the use of comparison to reach some particular end result.

However, it also has another definition: the combination of premises and conclusions in the pursuit of some sort of *truth*. Note that logic and truth are not mutually exclusive. The ideas of logic can be used as a foundation for nonsensical things. For example, if my argument were like so:

All dogs are blue

I have a dog

My dog is blue

These statements are logically sound just based on the fundamental structure of the argument. It is not, however, true because its premise of all dogs being blue is incorrect. However, this does mean that by extension that many things can be figured out in a logical manner and that we can use logic based upon truthful premises in order to figure out a truthful conclusion.

These logical premises, in the context of programming, are known as *comparisons*. Comparisons essentially take one thing and another thing and then compare them to something else in order to determine whether something is true.

For example, take 3 and 7; if I were to say that "3 is more than 7", this is a logical comparison between these two values. This entire statement would be false since 3 is not more than 7.

In programming, we can do this with any given variables and values that we want so long as they are comparable. You can even overload these operators in order to define new ways for things to be comparable when you start with C++ and similar languages.

For right now, though, let's focus on the things which allow us to compare values. These are known as *comparison operators*. The comparison operators in C and, by extension, Arduino is like so:

s == t

This checks to see whether or not s and t are equal.

s < t

This checks to see whether or not s is less than t.

s <= t

This checks to see whether or not s is less than or equal to t.

s > t

This checks to see whether or not s is more than t.

s >= t

This checks to see whether or not s is either greater than or equal to t.

s != t

This checks to see whether or not s is *not equal* to t.

One of these comparisons has two names: a *statement* and an *expression*. In programming, they're generally referred to as *expressions* in order to not confuse them with the computer science concept of the statement, but you can actually evaluate more than one of these expressions at once. This is known as *statement calculus*, and it occurs through the use of what are called *logical operators*.

There are many logical operators, but the ones in C that you most need to know are like so:

A && B

Checks to see if both expression A and expression B are true.

A || B

!*A*

Checks to see if the statement A is *not* true. If it is *not* true, then we will return true since the statement "not A" *is* true.

If you're familiar at all with discrete mathematics or symbolic logic, then you'll see quite easily how many of the concepts carry over from it. However, even if you aren't familiar, they're still very easy for you to grasp nonetheless.

Conditionals

Now that we've talked a bit about logic and truth, we can build on that knowledge to talk about what is called *conditional statements*. Conditional statements are one major part of control flow. Control flow is extremely prominent in computer science, and almost every application you've ever used will have some degree of control flow built into it. Control flow is, after all, the basic way that you can give your program some sort of "intelligence," if we're defining intelligence as the capacity to make decisions based off of given data.

These can take two forms: the passive and the active conditional. The passive conditional is the most basic form, so we're going to cover that first.

The passive conditional is called so because there is no obligation for the program to run the code of the conditional. For example, if the program gets to the conditional and the condition isn't met, the code is skipped altogether, and the program moves on to the next part of the program.

The passive conditional is established through the *if statement*. The if statement just evaluates whether or not a given condition is true and then will execute the code within the if statement's code block if it is true. Otherwise, the code block will be skipped entirely. The syntax for an if statement is like so:

if (condition) {

// code goes within

}

This is complemented by the *active conditional*. The active conditional is parallel to the passive conditional because it forces the program to execute *some* code even if the statement isn't true. So in essence, if the statement is true, then the code within *that* code block will run. Otherwise, an alternative code block that has been written will be executed. This is done through the *else* statement.

```
if (condition) {

// code goes within

} else {

// back-up code is here

}
```

However, you may realize that sometimes you want to test more than one condition. You can do this with the *else if* statement which is supposed to be sandwiched between your if and else statements. You can supply additional conditions to be tested if the initial condition tested doesn't turn out to be true. It will test conditions in sequence, and if none of them are true, then the else statement will execute. The syntax for an if statement is like so:

```
if (condition) {

} else if (condition) {

} else if (condition) {

} else {

}
```

With as many or as few else if statements as you really want there to be. There is no upward or downward bound so don't worry too much about that.

Loops

Loops are an essential part of programming. In the first book we only really covered for loops, but in this book, we're going to cover both for loops and while loops. Loop logic is an essential part of our daily lives, but a lot of the time we fail to consider how important it really is to things that we do every single day.

For example, consider the act of counting from 1 to 5. You start at the number one; you say the number out loud by forming your mouth into the proper shape and expelling air, then you add 1 to the number; this repeats until you reach the number 6. At the number 6, you see that we are now bigger than the number 5 so you no longer say the number aloud.

This is a relatively simple example, but it is an important one nonetheless because it really frames just how insidious and important loop logic is.

There are two different main forms of loops in C that you'll need to know: for loops and while loops. We're going to cover while loops first because they're far simpler in concept.

While loops are relatively simple to understand but they're harder to know when to use accurately. Much of the time, you're going to be using for loops just because they seem to have more obvious and immediate uses than while loops do.

With for loops, you have really obvious bounds, but with while loops, you don't. For this reason, while loops are best suited to those cases where you don't have an actual finite number of times for a loop to run.

A while loop simply checks a condition and then runs the code within the body of the loop for as long as that condition is met. If that condition is ever not met, then the loop will exit. Easy enough!

The syntax for a while loop is like so:

while (condition) {

// loop's internal code

}

While loops are best suited to the concept of the "game loop." These loops aren't exclusive to games, of course; they just express the idea of a game, because games will do the same thing over and over until a win or lose condition is met. When those conditions are met, the game is considered over.

The game loop is based on the idea of having either a true or false variable that is changed to the opposite when a certain condition is met. So, for example, the code may be:

#define TRUE 1

#define FALSE 0

int bHasWon = FALSE;

while (bHasWon == FALSE) {

// code goes here

}

Then have something that will change bHasWon to TRUE when the player wins. This will indicate that the loop should be terminated because the win condition has been met. Of course, this logic - again - can be used for many things aside from games. Anything with a central main menu will in fact likely use this sort of loop logic.

The other kind of loop is the *for* loop. The primary purpose of the for loop is to allow you to iterate through a given set of data with ease. For loops start with the creation of an iterator variable, which can be named whatever you want. The iteration step can be many things, but it normally is by 1 (*iterator++* or *iterator--* for +1 or -1 each time, respectively).

The syntax for a for loop is like so:

for (iterator declaration; condition; iteration step) {

// code goes within

}

So to print out every number in an array, we could do the following:

for (int i = 0; i < (sizeof(myArray)/sizeof(myArray[0]); i++)

{

printf("%s\n", myArray[i]);

}

Where sizeof(myArray)/sizeof(myArray[0]) gets the number of elements within the array altogether.

Functions

The last thing that we need to talk about and rehash before moving on to the next chapter is the concept of *functions*. Functions are a foundational concept in C programming and Arduino by extension. You're going to run into them a lot, so it is important that you understand exactly how they work. Fortunately, they aren't a very terribly difficult concept to understand! Functions simply are based around the idea of breaking something down into code which can be reused over and over.

Functions may be familiar to you through things like past math classes, where you would have something like f(x) = y. X was the argument, and the function manipulated x in order to give you the value y. Functions in computer science are relatively similar (and are very much similar to higher level functions in mathematics, but I'm not so willing to assume that everybody who reads this book has already worked with those, so I'm going to pull back on that one.)

Functions have a few basic parts. First, they have their declaration. In C, you either have to declare a new function at the start of the file, called prototyping, or you have to put it before your main function. For simplicity's sake, we'll go ahead and just prototype them at the start of our file and put them after our sketch's primary functions.

Functions also have a return type. This is the kind of value that they *give back* at the end of the function. So, for example, a function called *convertTemp* would probably give back a decimal number. Therefore, the type of function would be a *float* or a *double*.

Functions can also be written which *don't* have a return type. These functions are called *void* functions. They are valid, especially for performing certain operations that are to be done over and over but aren't particularly mathematical in and of themselves, like printing text to a serial or spinning a motor or something of the like.

Functions also have *arguments*. A function doesn't *have* to have arguments, but you can *give* a function an argument. A function's arguments are defined in its declaration. You can tell the types of the arguments as well as the placeholder names. You can then treat the arguments as variables within the body of the function and feed in the actual values when you call the function later in the program.

Again, though, a function doesn't necessarily *have* to have an argument. This isn't a requirement for a working function. Remember that as you go forward!

The syntax for prototyping a function is like so:

functionType functionName(arguments, if any);

And the syntax for actually writing a function is like so:

functionType functionName(arguments, if any) {

// code within the function

// return valueName if necessary;

}

So, let's make a function which will return the volume of a cone as a float. This is going to need two arguments, radius and height. It will be a double since we're working with pi and want it to be as accurate as possible. We will feed in doubles as arguments, too.

We could prototype the function near the start of our program like so:

double volumeOfCone(double radius, double height);

Then at some point in the program afterward, but not within another function, we could include the actual body of our function like so:

double volumeOfCone(double radius, double height) {

return 0.33333333 * 3.141569 * (radius * radius) * height;

}

We can then treat the return value of this function as a value of itself. So, we could create a double variable and assign the return value of this function to it:

double volumeOfConeRThreeHFive = volumeOfCone(3.00, 5.00);

This would return the volume of a cone with a radius of three and height of five and save it to the variable we created. We can also insert it anywhere that value is accepted, like in a printf statement or into a formatted string or something similar.

With that, we've covered the last thing that we needed to go back over before we get into some of the dense and meaty concepts within this book. In the chapters to follow, we're going to be going over much more in-depth programming concepts as we try to figure out the world of programming in Arduino at a greater level than we had before.

MORE IN-DEPTH COMPUTER SCIENCE TOPICS

See, working with computers - especially something so precise and hardware-limited as the Arduino - can be immensely rewarding, but if you want to be good at it, you have to have a very firm understanding of a lot of underlying concepts.

It is perfectly fine, for example, to understand what variables *are*, but if you don't understand how they *work*, you may end up wasting a lot of computing power with them when you really don't mean to. And again, when you're working with something like Arduino, that's the last thing that you want to do.

So, in this chapter, we're going to be building on some of our topics that we've already discussed so that you can be an all-around better Arduino programmer and, in turn, a better C/C++ programmer. By the end of this chapter, you're going to feel as though you have a firmer grasp on a lot of different concepts.

Memory Management and Pointers

The first thing that we're going to talk about in this chapter is the concept of memory management and pointers. This is an immensely important topic, especially when we're talking about Arduino. You don't have a lot of onboard memory to work with, so you need to make the best of what you have.

This can be a little tricky for newer programmers to grasp. In fact, it is tricky enough that in the first book, you were warned to stay away from this in particular. This is because it is a relatively high-level topic. After all, the very idea of pointers gets into some pretty low-level programming that you most likely haven't had any experience with.

Let's think back to a second to our discussion about data and data types. We talked about how you could create variables and all of the things that you can do with them. One thing we didn't really talk about, however, is how these variables work in terms of the computer's memory.

Computers store variables for running the length of a process called the *random-access memory*. You can think of random-access memory as space that can be allocated dynamically and as needed in accordance with the current demands of the program. All values which are worked with by the programmer and the program are stored, to some degree, in the random-access memory. Variables can be defined, which allocate a set space of random-access memory that is the size of the defined variable.

Variables, too, by their very nature, are essentially references to the places that a value sits within the computer's memory. When you refer to a variable, though, you aren't actually working with that *value* necessarily. For example, when you pass a variable to a function, you aren't sending the variable *itself*. Instead, you're sending a *copy* of the variable's value to be manipulated by the newer function. This copy is then disposed of when the function is finished.

In the olden days of computing, this made a bit of sense. After all, you don't necessarily want to *change* the value of some variables every time that you send those to a function. It makes sense for such a case *not to* be the default. Additionally, functions are also stored in the computer's memory in a certain way such that it makes more sense to send them values directly than to send them references to values elsewhere in memory. It makes them, in a manner of speaking, run more efficiently.

However, there are certainly cases where you would want to refer to the value of a variable itself and not just to the value that the variable *refers*. For these cases, you'd want to use pointers. Note at the same time that it is certainly possible to work through most Arduino sketches without ever having to use pointers. However, there are times where you will be working with a data structure or need to *create* a data structure, and in these cases, a working knowledge of pointers is very useful.

Not to mention that whether we're talking in terms of general programming and Arduino programming specifically, pointers are something you *need* to know because they are an important concept of *memory management*. You have to understand memory management in order to write efficient programs, and you need to at the very least understand the concept - if not for Arduino then for anything else that you want to program.

So, what are the key points to take away from all of this? Well, first and foremost, what are pointers? Pointers offer a method for you to refer to a value by its place in memory rather than just by a copy of its value. This is important why? Because it allows you to pass and work with direct values rather than simply copies of those values that you may have through variables. This is foundational to programming in C and will also probably come up sometimes during Arduino programs. While generally, you can write entire sketches without ever even using pointers, it is still good knowledge to have for when you are looking through other people's sketches and learning from the code that they're writing.

So, how do pointers *work* then? Pointers work through a combination of operators called *reference* and *dereference* operators. You can use these in order to create new pointer variables and point them toward an already existing variable.

The first thing that you're going to do is create a new pointer of to the type of value that you're wanting to point. You do this by using the reference operator *. So, for example, let's say we had this:

int apples = 3;

And we wanted to create a pointer that would point to this variable. The first thing that we would do is create a new pointer:

int *ptr;

You can put the reference operator wherever. Most prefer to stick it on the variable name, but others prefer to put it with the type. Others still put it equidistant between the two with a space between both. It depends on the coding conventions of whatever you're working with, but generally putting it with the variable name is a safe bet.

Afterward, what you're going to do is define to the address you want it to point. You do this through the *dereference* operator: &. You set the pointer variable *itself* to this, not the pointer variable with the reference operator. So, like this:

int *ptr;

ptr = &apples;

Then, whenever we go and modify the ptr variable through the reference operator, it will change the *value* stored at the address that we pointed it to. Like so:

*ptr = 4;

printf("%d", apples);

// this would print out *four* since we changed the value at the address referred to by the variable *apples* to be 4 rather than 3.

You can see pretty plainly how this would have a lot of utility to you as a programmer when you're trying to pass variables between functions and work with variables in a complex manner. Being able to directly manipulate pointers like this has a lot of useful perks, too. When you're working with a platform where memory is both as limited and as crucial as the Arduino, you're going to want to have at least the *ability* to work with memory directly. There are some more essential things that you will want to, but they are an advanced topic and aren't within the scope of this book. They also aren't particularly useful to Arduino programming itself, such as direct memory allocation through the *malloc* function.

Regardless, knowing how to work with pointers will push you forward as an Arduino programmer because when you do encounter pointers in the wild or have to create functions that pass variables that need to be directly modified, you can do so with ease and not be pulling your hair out in confusion.

Stacks

Stacks are yet another extremely important computer science concept. They're important primarily because they work in a really crucial and integral way with things like pointers and arrays. So, what are they?

This is a bit more in-depth than Arduino but, you will still inevitably run into the basic stack terminology in discussions on Arduino programming, so it is important that you have a solid idea of what the stack is and how it can be used.

"Stack" is actually a relatively versatile term. The idea of a "stack" simply refers to what it sounds like - a stack of values. You can add variables to this stack. Imagine a block tower. This is essentially how a stack works.

You can put things on top of the stack, and these things are also the first things to be *removed* from the stack. This is especially useful in algorithmic programming, but it does bear some use in Arduino programming as well. Why? Because when you're dealing with complex and limited memory structures, you're going to inevitably run into many occasions where the best path forward is to use a stack. This is because the stack is very memory-easy. It doesn't demand anything aside from the location of the last thing in the stack and the current thing in the stack, and these things are easy to use.

It also gives you an incredibly easy way to refer back to data that you've already used, so that's pretty nifty in and of itself. Stacks are, in essence, an extremely useful tool for any programmer, and there are some Arduino IDE functions that actually reference the concept of a stack and build on the concept.

The stack is built of two essential functions: pushing and popping. Both are extremely easy to understand, so we shouldn't need to spend too much time going over what they actually are.

Pushing refers to adding something *to* the stack. It is a pretty straightforward concept. You can push a value onto the stack in order to save it for later and instantly recall it without having to worry about things such as the *name* of the variable on top of the stack or its value.

Popping refers to taking something *off* of the stack. When you pop a value from a stack, you remove the thing that was most recently added to the stack and take its value. You can then use its value however you like. If you want to return the value to the stack, just remember that you're going to have to *push* it on there again. When you pop something from the stack and remove it, the second-to-last thing that was pushed is now the first thing to be popped.

Again, the stack is a relatively simple concept, but it is nonetheless incredibly important to the overall idea of computer science as well as building and expanding your horizons in order to be better programming in general.

Structures

One of the nuances of Arduino programming and C in general that a lot of people don't take the time to learn as a newer programmer is the idea of *structures*. Structures are a relatively well-kept secret, but they can be incredibly useful.

Perhaps you've heard the term *object-oriented programming*. Structures in C were in many ways' precursors to the idea of object-oriented programming. While they aren't able to be anywhere near as extensively programmed as object-oriented concepts are able to be, they do offer a brilliant way for a programmer to group certain ideas together into a singular structure.

So, what exactly is a structure? Providing some definition for it will help you to get a better idea of how you can use it. Many times, there are concepts in programming that would make a lot more sense if you were to bundle them by putting them together. A great example is to think of a cat. You may need to work with several different *ideas* of a cat in your program, and for that, you'd be defining all sorts of different variables even though they all have a bunch of features in common. So, instead of doing this:

cat1Legs = 4;

cat2Legs = 4;

cat3Legs = 4;

cat1Color = 'brown';

cat2Color = 'black';

cat3Color = 'white with black spots';

cat1Breed = 'tabby';

cat2Breed = 'persian';

cat3Breed = 'american shorthair';

You can just define all of these in a single way and then work with them at a later point by accessing their *member data*. You do this through the use of a period. The syntax for defining a structure in C is like so:

struct NameOfStruct {

// data within struct

};

So, using the cat example:

struct MyCat {

int numberOfLegs;

String color;

String breed;

};

You could then define cats like so:

MyCat cat1 = {4, 'brown', 'tabby'};

MyCat cat2 = {4, 'black', 'persian'};

MyCat cat3 = {4, 'white with black spots', 'american shorthair'};

You can see how this presents the programmer with a much easier way to group important data together. There's a good chance you aren't going to be using this data *super* often, but it does allow you to have such a way to *do* this. It is important that you know what it is because you will eventually see it.

All of these concepts are important to Arduino because Arduino is far more restricted in terms of memory and processing power than your home computer would be. It is important that you know how to use these concepts so that you can make the most out of your Arduino's processing ability as well as write simpler and more elegant sketches than you would have otherwise. For example, you could create a structure that held three-byte variables called r, g, and b in order to program your RGB colors alongside the same lines in a simple manner. You could define new colors doing this to access them easily later on in your program, like so:

struct color {

byte r, g, b;

};

color blue = {0, 0, 255};

See how simple that is? But the utility of doing such a thing is pretty plainly obvious!

In this chapter, we've covered three major programming concepts that you're going to inevitably come across when you're working with other people's Arduino code and learning from what they've written, so it was important that I develop your ability to parse and work with these ideas.

ARDUINO API FUNCTIONS

In this chapter, we're going to start going into a lot of detail on functions that are provided by the Arduino API. The first book had a lot to do with the bare fundamentals of programming. This is great and all, but we didn't really get too much experience with the Arduino API itself. Our goal now is to get some experience with the numerous functions that are provided by the Arduino interface for programmers to use.

The Arduino API is the rich set of different things that are provided to the hopeful Arduino programmer to give them more options in their programming. The Arduino team has done a fantastic job of providing a full-featured API that gives the programmer a large variety of different things that they can do within the context of their Arduino tinkering.

We're going to be dividing these by section and going into a lot more information on each function, so settle in tight. What you get from this chapter is a full reference on Arduino programming that you can swing back to whenever you need.

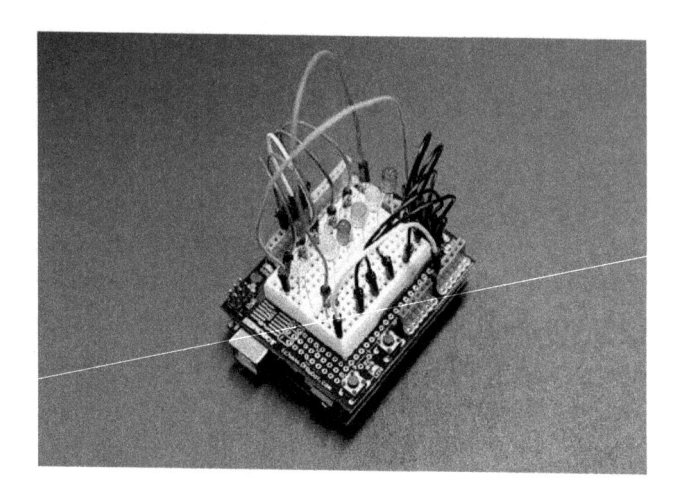

Digital Input and Output

There are a number of functions defined by the Arduino API in order to allow you to work with digital pins. This section is dedicated to those functions, three in particular.

pinMode(pin, INPUT - OUTPUT - or INPUT_PULLUP)

This allows you to specify a given pin and then designate whether that pin will act as an *input* or act as an *output*. Newer Arduino models are able to have pins enabled through pullup resistors using the INPUT_PULLUP mode.

Analog Input and Output

On top of the digital pins, you also have your analog pins. These functions are intended to read voltage from a given pin, always between 0 and 5 volts. The upper range will be closer to *1023* while the lower will be closer to *0*.

analogRead(pin)

This will read the voltage from a given pin and return it as an integer from 0 to 1023.

analogReference(type)

This will configure the voltage to be used as a reference depending upon the type of your Arduino.

Most of the time, you can specify "type" as DEFAULT or INTERNAL. There are a few cases where you'll want to specify a different reference voltage.

analogWrite(pin, value)

This will write a given voltage valued from 0 to 1023, with 1023 being 4.99999 volts and 0 being 0 volts.

Advanced Input and Output

These don't really fall under either the digital or analog categories, but they're more advanced input and output categories that will allow you to do more in general with your Arduino board.

*tone(*pin, frequency, OPTIONAL duration*)*

This allows you to specify a given frequency and then generate a square wave of that frequency on a given pin.

noTone(pin)

This will stop the tone being generated by the tone function.

pulseIn(pin, value)

This will allow you to read the pulse of a given pin. If the pin is fluctuating from high to low, then it will return the time in microseconds between the high and low. Because pulses may not be completely even, you can actually specify whether you want it to read the HIGH pulse (the time for the HIGH value to change to LOW) or the LOW pulse (the time for the LOW value to change to HIGH).

pulseInLong(pin, value)

This is just like the function before, but instead of returning an integer number of microseconds, it will return a *long* number of microseconds, which essentially offers a much larger time dimension for which you can receive data.

*shiftIn(*dataPin, clockPin, bitOrder*)*

This will send a byte's worth of data to a given pin, bit by bit. The data pin is the pin where you're going to be sending each bit, the clock pin is the pin which will designate that dataPin has read data, and the bitOrder can be either MSBFIRST or LSBFIRST (Most significant or least significant bit first, respectively.)

shiftOut(dataPin, clockPin, bitOrder, value)

This is much like the function before, but it allows you to *send* data to a pin one bit at a time. Everything else is the same, but you can send out data using the *value* argument. The value argument must be of the type *byte*.

Time

These functions are intended to help you in working with time-sensitive things in the Arduino scope.

delay(value)

This allows you to pause your sketch for a certain amount of time specified by the integer *value* in milliseconds.

delayMicroseconds(value)

This is functionally the same as the delay() function except for the fact that it uses microseconds instead of milliseconds.

Math

Believe it or not, programming sometimes involves a lot of math. The math functions in the Arduino API are similar in many ways to those math functions defined by the C math library, but they keep you from having to import any additional mathematical libraries. Even if you don't use much math in your program, you'll still benefit from knowing that these exist because you never know when you might need them.

abs(value)

This function returns the absolute value of a given number or the distance between zero and a given number on a number line.

constrain(variant, lowerBound, upperBound)

This allows you to create a function such that a number will always be within the lower and upper bound.

map(number, fromMin, fromMax, toMin, toMax)

This will map a number from one range to another range.

max(number1, number2)

Will return the highest number of number1 or number2. Simple enough!

min(number1, number2)

Pretty much the exact opposite of the max function. This will return the lowest of the two numbers.

pow(base, exponent)

This will allow you to take a given number and then raise it to an exponent. C, which doesn't have a built in exponential operator, makes great use of this function.

sq(number)

This will return the square of a given number. A shorthand for *pow(number, 2)*.

sqrt(number)

This will calculate the square root of a given number.

cos(angle)

This will compute the cosine of a given angle, with the angle to be specified in radians.

sin(angle)

This will compute the sin of a given angle, with the angle to be specified in radians.

tan(angle)

This will compute the tangent of a given angle, with the angle to be specified in radians.

Characters

While they will be rare, it is important that you have a set of functions primed for you to use whenever you're working with character sets.

isAlpha(character)

This will return whether or not the character is alphabetical.

isAlphaNumeric(character)

This will return whether or not the character is either alphabetic or numeric.

isAscii()

This will return whether or not the character is an ASCII character.

isControl()

This will return whether or not a character is a control character.

isDigit()

This will return whether or not a character is a number.

isGraph()

This will return whether or not the character is something that has visual data. A space, for example, does not have visual data.

isHexadecimalDigit()

This will return whether or not the character is hexadecimal.

isLowerCase()

This will return whether or not the character is lowercase.

isPrinable()

This will return whether or not the character can be printed to the console.

isPunct()

This will return whether or not the character is a punctuation mark.

isSpace()

This will return whether or not the character is a space.

isUpperCase()

This will return whether or not the character is in upper case.

isWhiteSpace()

This will return whether or not the character is a whitespace character, like a tab, space, or line break.

Random Numbers

These functions will allow you to create random numbers in your program. Note that computers can never be truly random and spontaneous; all things are based on inputs, and nothing will ever be without these inputs in a computer. As a result, the random function *must* be seeded.

randomSeed(number)

This starts the random number generator. You feed a number in, and it starts at some random point within the sequence of the pseudo-random number generator's numerical sequence.

random(OPTIONAL minimum, maximum)

This will act as the bounds to your random number generation. The maximum value is the highest random number that you will allow, and the minimum input is the lowest value you will allow. If you don't specify a minimum, then the minimum will be assumed to be 0.

Bitwise Functions

These functions allow you to work with bits and bytes, which are the smallest pieces of data that a computer will work with. You can, theoretically, work with smaller values (in terms of overall computing power required), but these are the smallest practical values that you're going to work with while programming for Arduino.

bit(bitNum)

This will return the value of a given bit.

bitClear(variable, bit)

This will set the given *bit* of a specified numeric *variable* to 0.

bitRead(variable, bit)

This will give back the *bit* of a specified numeric *variable*.

bitSet(variable, bit)

This will set a given *variable's bit* as position denoted by *bit* to 1.

bitWrite(variable, bit, 0 or 1)

This will set the *bit* at the given position within the *variable* to either 0 or 1, depending on what you say.

highByte(value)

This will return the highest byte of a given value.

lowByte(value)

This will return the *lowest* byte of a given value.

USING THE STREAM CLASS (AND WORKING WITH STRINGS)

This deserved its own chapter. While this also deals heavily with using the Arduino API in an effective manner, this is such a broad lesson that we really needed to break it into its own chapter so that we could properly discuss it.

The stream class is a relatively simple concept to grasp. The stream class in itself is based on using reading information from a certain source and using this within your sketch. Because the stream is about reading data, it is necessary that we also talk about working with the keyboard and mouse in this chapter even though these aren't related *intrinsically* to the stream class.

When you're working with data, especially reading in data, you're going to inevitably find times that you're going to need to work with sets of characters like words or sentences or anything of that nature. The idea of *strings* presents you the opportunity to do this.

Strings are basically just sets of character values that are linked together as an array. Therefore, they're contiguous in memory, and the computer sees them as one large and interconnected unit. Working with strings means learning to manipulate these units to the best of your ability.

It is really simple in and of itself. Strings are essentially just *character arrays*. This means that we're technically working with what are called *C-style Strings*, which are basically strings that have a very low level of abstraction. For example, in a lot of more modern and higher-level languages, strings aren't revealed in their character as a character array; they're rather treated as a more abstract object, even if they *are* a character array at their core.

A string is composed of the *n+1* characters, where *n* is the number of letters within the string in a general sense. So, for example, the size of a string for the word "hello" would be *six* characters. The reason it is n+1 is that the string ends in a null terminating character, \0, which indicates that the end of the array has been reached and properly terminates it.

You can define a string in the same way that you would an array. You can also make them bigger than the string that they're going to contain. When you define an array, you may give it a value right off the bat, but you can also just define their size and expand them at a later point. This also makes strings, in one manner or another, dynamic and able to be changed at a later point in the program by rewriting the data within the string.

This information is of great use to you as a programmer because strings are a fundamental part of any sort of program that handles information, especially those which handle file input and output.

We've already spent a bit of time rehashing information from the book prior, but just for the sake of clarity, we're going to go ahead and define a string:

char myString[6] = "hello";

You can then refer to this entire string at a later point by the name of the character. Most of the data that is worked with by the Arduino will be worked with in terms of bytes, and most actual textual data will be worked with in terms of C strings because characters are tremendously easy to parse.

It is important that we cover all of this so that we can actually develop an idea of how to treat strings in the context of Arduino programming alongside everything that we're going to be working on through this book.

Serial

While you can't necessarily implement the stream class itself, you can implement its *derivatives*, and this is where you start to find a whole lot of utility. The serial class is an extension of the stream class that allows the Arduino board to communicate with other devices such as a computer.

Serial is enacted through both the Serial port on the Arduino as well as the USB link to the computer. In this section, we're going to be outlining all of the different functions which make up the

Serial class so that you can make the absolute most of this invaluable resource.

if (Serial)

Serial.begin(rate)

You're already familiar with this function. It allows you to start the serial transmission of data. You can specify the specific rate of data transmission in bits per second.

Serial.end()

This allows you to end serial communication. You can later restart the serial communication by calling the Serial.begin() function if you wish. While the serial communication is disabled, you can use the serial pins for generalized entry and exit of data.

Serial.find(string)

This will search for the given string within the data provided by the Serial. If the string is found, the method will return true. If the string is not found, the method will return false.

Serial.findUntil(string, OPTIONAL endString)

This will look for the string within the serial buffer until either the string is found or a specified terminating string is found. If the target string is found, then the method will return true. If the terminating string is found or if the method times out, it will return false.

Serial.flush()

This will allow you to halt processes until all data being sent to the serial has been sent. Straightforward!

Serial.parseFloat()

This will return the first floating point number to be provided by the serial stream. It will be brought to an end by any character that isn't a floating point.

Serial.parseInt()

This will return the first integer number to be provided by the serial stream. It will be brought to an end by the first character that isn't a digit.

Serial.peek()

This will return the very next character to be imported by the serial buffer. However, it will not remove the character from the buffer. This makes it fundamentally different from the Serial.read() method we'll be getting to momentarily. This means that you can simply see what character is coming next.

Serial.print(value, OPTIONAL format)

You can specify the format, optionally. Otherwise, integers will print as decimals by default; floats will print to two decimal places by default, and so forth.

You can send characters or strings as is to the print statement and it will print them without any issue.

Serial.println(value, OPTIONAL format)

This will allow you to print out values just like you would with the normal print method

Serial.read()

This will read in the data which is coming in through the serial port. Simple enough! It is added to an incoming stream of serial data called the serial buffer. When you read from this buffer, the information is destroyed, so be sure to save the data to a variable if you need to reuse it at some point.

Serial.readBytes(serialBuffer, numberOfBytes)

This will read in characters from the serial port to a buffer. You can determine the number of bytes that are to be read. Your buffer must be either a char array or a byte array.

Serial.readBytesUntil(terminatorCharacter, serialBuffer, numberOfBytes)

This will read in characters from the serial either until the given number of bytes has been read or until a given terminating character has been read. In either case, the method will terminate.

Serial.write()

This will write data to the serial port; however, this particular method only sends binary data to the serial port. If you need to send ASCII data, you should use the print method instead.

Serial.serialEvent()

Whenever data comes to be available for use by the serial port, this function will be called. You can then use the Serial.read() function in order to read in data from the serial port.

With that, we've covered a lot of the particular functions related to the serial class and how it pertains to programming with the Arduino API. The next thing that we're going to need to work with is the Ethernet class.

USER DEFINED FUNCTIONS

One of the ways you can help keep your code neat, organized, and modular (reusable) is to use functions in your code. Additionally, they help make your code smaller by making certain sections reusable. Functions are like tools that were created to serve a particular function, as the name suggests.

While we have already encountered a few user-defined functions, we will cover them in greater detail now and explain some of the features we may have glossed over when we encountered them last time. Let's look at the declaration of a function now:

float employeeEarnings (float hoursWorked, float payRate) {

float result;// this will be the value we return when this function is called. It should match the datatype before our function name.

result = hoursWorked * payRate

return result//   return tells the function to send a value   back once to where it was called

}

This function clearly takes two arguments, hoursWorked, and payRate, both of which are 'floats.' It does some simple math on them and then returns a float as a value. Return means to terminate the function and send back whatever value is placed after the word return, usually a variable, as the result of some calculations.

Let's see us call this function now to get an employee's earnings:

```
void loop () {
floathoursWorked = 37.5;
float payRate= 18.50;
float result = employeeEarnings (hoursWorked, payRate)
// result will be 693.75
```

First, the function must be declared outside of any other functions. This means you need to write the code for the function you are creating outside of either setup() or loop(), or any other user-defined function.

Let's see another example that sample sketch that could be used to smooth sensor readings:

```
int sensorSmoothing (analogPin) {
int sensorValue = 0;
for (int index = 0; index < 5, index++)
digitalWrite(LED_BUILTIN, HIGH);   //Turn on LED for
        smoothing
sensorValue = sensorValue + analogRead(analogPin)
delay(100)// 100 millisecond delay between samples
}
digitalWrite(LED_BUILTIN, LOW);//turn off LED
```

sensorValue = sensorValue / 5// average the values over five samples

return sensorValue;

}

This kind of function can be used for smoothing the data input of many sensors if they are prone to jittery inputs. This will average the samples to give a more consistent flow of data. You can see that this code is very similar to our last example:

void loop () {

int sensorPin = 0;// analog pin 0

int sensorValue = sensorSmoothing (sensorPin);

}

Here, when we try to initialize our sensorValue variable it will call the sensorSmoothing() function on analog pin 0, and return the average result over five samples)

Functions do not always need to have parameters or return variables either. Sometimes functions can return no value and have no parameters. All they do is execute a few lines of code and then terminate bringing the compiler back to place in the code they were called.

CONCLUSION

The next step is to get out there and start making your own sketches! Go to your local hobby store to get some ideas or go to the community to see what new projects you might want to try. After you have an idea where you might want to go next, (robots are pretty fun!) join the community! Seriously, it is a lot of fun to build projects with friends and compare them with each other. If you feel like you don't know where to start, don't worry! There are many online sources that share coding and techniques to improve your game. Many online sites also have forums specifically tailored to helping people like you learn and show off what they have done. It is also a fantastic way to learn and grow as a hobbyist.

If you want to get started but are feeling strapped for cash, there are options. Like we've said above, there are fairly cheap modules for purchase on the Arduino site and others. Also, cheaper programming languages are available, and some are even free. Learning these languages are actually easier than you would think. If you know one programming language, the rest are easier to understand and write. There are also books at your local library that will help you learn how to code. Many libraries offer interlibrary loans, which means that you can learn about programming from books from all around you! Best of all, learning from a book from the library is absolutely free! If you have any questions about this, remember that you can go online and find others who have worked with Arduino and know how to get you started.

Arduino board can be programmed to light or fade a LED etc. The syntax used in Arduino programming is similar to C++. If you are good at C++, then programming in Arduino will be easy for you. The variables in Arduino are initialized within the setup() function. The loop() section has the block to be run repeatedly. When working with Arduino pins, you must specify the pin you need to work with. The pins are normally identified with numbers as each has a unique number. After getting the board, you have to setup Arduino IDE on your computer. This is where you will be writing your Arduino code before uploading bit to the board. Arduino code is commonly known as a sketch. You must get a source of power. However, some board types must be configured to allow power to be drawn from a computer. The effect of a sketch on the board will be seen after uploading it to the board, in which one has to click the Upload button.

There are many sensors and additions to each Arduino, so make sure you check out which you would like to employ. The great part of owning an Arduino is that you'll get the chance to try many experiments. You're not just limited to what the sensors can read, either. Come up with some ways on your own to make the machines work for you. Try programming simple requests first—like setting up blinking lights or figuring out how Arduino can monitor inputs—and see what you can do from there. I have included many Arduino codes for you to use, but feel free to find some of your own! There are many guides for help.

You can also check out some more advanced concepts we didn't have a chance to touch on here such as headers, classes, changing the clock speed for the chip, adding cores, adding libraries, there is so much that you can do with this chip, it really is incredible. Pick a direction that interests you and see where it takes you. I hope that this guide has offered you some small inspiration to go out there and try new things and see what your sketch designing skills are capable of.

Finally, thank you for finishing this book! Arduinos are a fun way to get started on your programming journey. Since you've purchased this book, we hope you've grown, and if you found this book useful in any way, a review on Amazon is always appreciated!

REFERENCES

Arduino Reference. (2019). Retrieved from https://www.arduino.cc/reference/en/language/structure/comparison-operators/lessthan/

What is an Arduino? - learn.sparkfun.com. (2019). Retrieved from https://learn.sparkfun.com/tutorials/what-is-an-arduino/all#the-arduino-family

ARDUINO PROGRAMMING

The Ultimate Intermediate Guide
To Learn Arduino Programming
Step By Step

RYAN TURNER

INTRODUCTION

Congratulations on taking the next step and purchasing *Arduino Programming: The Ultimate Intermediate Guide to Learn Arduino Programming Step By Step*. The goal of this book is to extend the knowledge you already built up using the previous book in the series.

Progressing from the beginner level to intermediary is no easy task, as many students give up due to the pressure involved in working with hardware, coding patterns, and various tools. You took this step, and this book will reward you for it by guiding you to the next level. You will learn how to build interesting projects using the Arduino board, and you will also be working with real world application examples.

The main purpose of *Arduino Programming: The Ultimate Intermediate Guide to Learn Arduino Programming Step By Step* is to give you all the tools you need to build more powerful projects and applications. You will learn how to improve your programming and how to improve your Arduino projects by boosting its power and using various modules. You will learn how to apply and code those modules to create advanced storage systems, networks, and even an Arduino global positioning system.

This book will guide you step by step through all the techniques, concepts, and tools you need. There will also be real world examples through which you will learn how to make the right connections, and how to implement your code. Project-based work is the best kind of work when it comes to learning more advanced topics.

How to Benefit the Most

As already mentioned, this book isn't just about theory. In every chapter and every section, you will encounter real world projects and study them step by step. You will learn how to connect physical modules to the Arduino, and how to write the firmware so that they function properly. This means that in order to benefit from this book, you have to practice alongside with it. Do not skip over practical examples, as they are crucial to understand the implementation of various techniques in other projects.

The practical examples contained in this book are real world projects that rely on widely available electronics and software components. Don't worry about the budget, because all of the modules you will work with are cheap and readily available in any electronics store. The programming part of the projects is also easy to understand, and even if you encounter difficulties, it is easy to research outside of this guide. All of the code, libraries, and applications can be found in a large number of places, as they are open source and used to teach students all over the world. If you get stuck, don't be afraid to join an online community of Arduino enthusiasts. You can learn a lot more with help from those who have the same interests as you. Plus, it's much more fun to work on a project when you can talk about it to others who understand you.

With that being said, you'll get the most benefit out of this book by putting everything you learn into practice. The key here is practice, practice, practice!

CHAPTER 1: PROGRAMMING IMPROVEMENTS

No matter the project, you need to prepare your work environment and think about the elements that will make your code logical, readable, and simply beautiful to look at. In this chapter we are going to discuss improving your programming with functions, math, and calculation optimization.

In the previous book, *Arduino Programming: The Ultimate Beginner's Guide to Learn Arduino Programming Step by Step*, we discussed the basics of programming as well as Arduino functions, however we didn't go into too much detail. In this chapter we will explore them further, and build on your knowledge of mathematics and trigonometry as well.

Functions

In this section we are going to go over the basics to refresh your memory, because we need to later dive into more detail. The foundation is extremely important, especially because we need to go over mathematical and trigonometric functions soon.

As you should already know, a function simply refers to code that can be used and reused from any section of the program. In a program written in C, a function has a unique name, it is global and can require arguments, as well as return results.

With the Arduino IDE a function prototype can be created automatically, however sometimes we have to declare it ourselves.

This can be done in one single code file in the beginning. For instance, let's say we want a function that returns the sum of two integers as a result. We will have two variables that are integers, and therefore our result will also be an integer. Here's the example in code:

int mySum (int x, int y);

Now that we have our basic prototype, we can see that it is identical to the header. The function's header is simply the first statement definition. Here's how the structure of the function looks:

int mySum (int x, int y) // the header

{

    // the body

}

The general structure of the header is simply returnType functionName (arguments). The returnType is a variable, and when the function doesn't return any result we need to state it as equal to void. The functionName can be any name you choose, just make sure to always use an easy to understand name that describes what the function is all about. Keep in mind that code readability is crucial to a clean and improved code, so you don't want to have functions such as mathFunction1. In case you weren't aware, Arduino, as well as C, respects the Camelcase naming convention, so label your functions like "mySum" for instance. As for the arguments, they are just variable declarations that are in fact optional. You don't always have to declare the arguments, especially when you want a function to result in an action that is always the same.

The function's body is where we find all the detailed instructions. You can simply refer to it as "the code" because this is where everything happens. Variables are defined, conditions are laid, and loops come out to play. Now let's take the mySum function and give it a body:

int mySum (int x, int y) // the header

{

    int result;   // the variable that contains our result

    result = x + y; // the operation is performed and then stored in the result

    return result;   // returns the result

}

Now let's take a look at an Arduino code example of the same process:

void setup() {

Serial.begin (9600) ; An awesome example of Arduino code

}

Void loop() {

int currentResult;

for (int i = 0 ; in < 100 ; i++)

{

    currentResult = mySum (i, i + 1);

    Serial.println (currentResult)

}

Delay (2000) ; perform a pause for 2 seconds

}

int mySum (int x, int y)

{

    int result;

    result = x + y;

    return result;

The code should be self-explanatory, but the most important aspect of this example is that we make the call first and the function follows with the return of the result from the calculation. In other words, a function's "call" statement that returns a result is a value.

Now that we quickly recapped the basics of functions, let's discuss what the benefits are and why we should always use them.

The Benefits of Functions

As already mentioned, code needs to be readable and well-structured. If you are still a beginner programmer, you might be tempted to stick to the basics and avoid functions. This is a grave mistake, and you should use functions as much as possible in order to split your code into optimal segments. With that being said, here are the advantages of using functions and how they can improve your programming skills:

1. **Easier coding and readability**: Stay organized with clean code. When you first write your code, you will often use a lot of common statements that repeat themselves. The general rule accepted by most programmers is that if you write something more than twice, it's time to turn it into a function. You should never repeat yourself. You will also have a much easier time debugging your code. Instead of checking individual statements, you can simply debug the function and everything within it with be fixed.

2. **Reusability**: You will always have sections of code that are for general use and frequently needed, and higher level code that is rarely needed. For instance, you might create a function that converts Euros to US Dollars. This is a general purpose function that you might call very often. However, you might also create a function that converts USD into Norwegian Crowns, but it is rarely needed. The point is that in both cases you are reusing code, meaning that whenever the case arises you have a prepared function that simply needs to be called. Reusable code cuts down on your programming time so that you can focus on other tasks.

Mathematical Functions and Arduino

Mathematical functions are part of the C standard library and will work with Arduino as well. Many of these functions are also inherited in C++, however there are some differences when it comes to complex numbers. In C++ complex number handling isn't provided by the C library, but instead from its own which uses the following class template:

std: : complex

Take note, all of the mathematical functions will work well with floating point numbers. In C, the library is math.h and it needs to be called inside a program's header. Once it's mentioned, we can call any mathematical functions we need, such as the trigonometric functions.

Trigonometric Functions

In many cases, we have to perform trigonometric calculations in order to determine a distance which an object travelled, angular speed, and so on. Often, these operations need to take place inside the Arduino core, especially when you need to use it as an autonomous unit without a computer around. The basic trigonometric functions are provided inside the core, so let's discuss them briefly. A large part of the functions will return a radian as a result, because it is a unit that is used by most of them. Therefore, you should have some knowledge about radians, degrees, how to perform a conversion operation, and trigonometry in general.

A radian is the unit of measure for angles, and it is often used instead of degrees. For instance, a circle that measures in 360 degrees measures in slightly more than 6 radians. A degree is 1/360 of a circle, and since a circle can be measured as 2π, we can perform the conversion easily like so:

angle radian = angle degree * $\pi/180$

angle degree = angle radian * 180/π

Now let's define the sine, cosine, and tangent, with x being the angle measured in radians:

Sin(x) = opposite / hypotenuse

Cos(x) = adjacent / hypotenuse

Tan(x) = sin(x) / cos(x) = opposite / adjacent

Keep in mind that the sine and cosine go from a value of angles measured in radians of -1 to 1. The tangent, on the other hand, has certain points where it lacks a definition and therefore it evolves cyclically from negative infinity to positive infinity. The functions infinitely oscillate and we can use them for pure operations. Now that we can determine the sine, cosine, and tangent when there's an angle, let's establish how to determine the angle when we have the sine, cosine, and tangent.

In the scenario just mentioned, we need to use inverse trigonometric functions, namely the arcsine, arccosine, and arctangent. Here we have the inverse process of the previous functions, however they can supply us with many angles. Let's say we have a y integer and write the following mathematical connections:

sin (A) = x ó A = arcsin(x) + 2kπ or y = π − arcsin(x) + 2kπ

cos (A) = x ó A = arccos(x) + 2kπ or y = 2π − arccos (x) + 2kπ

tan (A) = x ó A = arctan(x) + kπ

Next, let's see the trigonometric function's prototype that can be found inside the Arduino core as well as the math.h library:

double sin (double x); returns the sine of x radians

double cos (double x); returns the cosine of x radians

double tan (double x); returns the tangent of x radians

double asin (double x); returns A, the angle corresponding to sin (A) = x

double acos (double x); returns A, the angle corresponding to cos (A) = x

double atan (double x); returns A, the angle corresponding to tan (A) = x

double atan2 (double y, double x); returns arctan (y/x)

When we need to perform mathematical calculations, we don't always rely on the trigonometric functions. Even for a simple operation, we can use exponential functions (and others), which are provided by Arduino as well. Here are some of the most common ones that you will use:

double pow (double x, double y); returns x to power y

double exp (double x); returns the exponential value of x

double log (double x); returns the natural logarithm of x with x > 0

double log10 (double x); returns the logarithm of x to base 10 with x > 0

double square (double x); returns the square of x

double sqrt (double x); returns the square root of x with x >= 0

double fabs (double x); returns the absolute value of x

So why would we use these operations? Let's say you are working on a basic Arduino project and you need to use a sensor to measure the temperature. You might be tempted to simply work with the inputs and outputs and not even make any conversions because it's not truly necessary. However, you can use these functions to achieve your goal and even optimize the firmware. With that being said, let's discuss calculation optimization.

Calculation Optimizations

In this section we aren't going to discuss all of the advanced programming optimization techniques, but we will explore methods of optimizing on pure calculations.

As you already know, the process of developing a project involves three steps: design, coding, and optimization. However, these development stages aren't as valid when it comes to small programs. Simpler projects are optimized directly in the coding process. This means that with each line of code you write, you should be thinking how you can optimize it. With that being said, do not sacrifice code readability just so you can fulfill various optimization processes.

Bit Shift Operations

Let's take an array as a simple example for calculation optimization. You might be inclined to use a multiplication operation when you perform the array indexing. However, doing so is extremely hard on your CPU resources, so you should seek to optimize. The easiest solution is to simply opt for working with an array declared with a power of two size, such as 512 instead of 500. Let's explore the "why."

People are taught to think in the decimal numeral system, meaning you count as follows: 0, 1, 2, 3, 4, 5, 6, 7, 8, 9, 10, etc. Computers, on the other hand, think in a binary numeral system instead, and they count as follows: 0, 1, 10, 11, 100, 101, 110, 111, etc. With that in mind, let's discuss the four bitwise operators:

Bitwise AND: We write this operator with an ampersand, "&" and it operates on every single bit position by following these rules:

0 & 0 == 0

0 & 1 == 0

1 & 0 == 0

1 & 1 == 1

Now let's see an example using integers:

int x = 35; // 00000000 00100011 in binary

int y = 49; // 00000000 00110001 in binary

int z = x & y; // 00000000 00100001 in binary, and 33 in decimal

Keep in mind that an integer has a 16-bit value. In our example we are comparing each bit, one at a time, for every position, based on the operator's rules.

Bitwise OR: This operator is represented by a vertical line "|". Here are the rules by which it operates on every single bit position:

0 | 0 == 0

0 | 1 == 1

1 | 0 == 1

1 | 1 == 1

Bitwise XOR: This operator is represented by a single caret "^" and it operates on every single bit position like so:

0 ^ 0 == 0

0 ^ 1 == 1

1 ^ 0 == 1

1 ^ 1 == 0

Bitwise NOT: This operator is represented by the tilde symbol "~". It can only be applied to a single number, meaning that it is a unary operator. Basically, it swaps every bit to its own opposite, like so:

~ 0 == 1

~ 1 == 0

Here's how an example with integers looks:

int x = 35; // 00000000 00100011 in binary

int y = ~x; // 11111111 11011100 (opposite of x), and -36 in decimal

Now that you know about bitwise operators, let's continue with the bit shift operation, which is the main attraction in this section.

The left shift operator is represented by "<<" and the right shift operator is represented by ">>". Now let's see how it is applied in a real example:

int x = 36; // 00000000 00100100

int y = x << 2; // 00000000 10010000, 144

int z = x >> 1; // 00000000 00010010, 18

As you may have worked out on your own, we have shifted the bits from a number of positions to the left, or to the right. You may have also noticed that performing << 1 is the same as multiplying by two, and >> is the same as dividing by two.

Bitwise operations are all about performance. They are primitive and supported directly by the computer's processors, especially when it comes to embedded systems. Using bitwise operations can significantly boost your performance and cause a much smaller resource drain. You should use the power of two as the array size because it will push the use of bit shift operators internally while the processor will perform the index calculations. Since multiplications and divisions can be easily done using a bit shift, you should eventually replace all of them that are by the power of two with bit shifting. Working with this type of operation will still keep your code clean and readable enough while also optimizing it.

Lookup Tables

Pay attention to the use of lookup tables, as they are one of the best tools at your disposal while programming. A lookup table is an array that consists of predetermined values. This means that resource heavy runtime calculations are replaced with an array index operation that is much simpler and easier to process. Imagine the following scenario. Your job is to track an object's location by using sensors to determine the distance. This means you will rely mostly on trigonometric calculations and perhaps power calculations as well. They are heavy resource consumers, therefore your processor will have to allocate a lot of power to perform these functions. Luckily, the easiest solution is to use array content reading instead of performing those mathematical calculations.

Lookup tables are simply stored inside a static program's memory once they are pre-calculated. You can also calculate them during a program's initialization stage. This method is a variation that is known as a pre-fetched lookup table.

The key is to pay attention to the functions that are draining the CPU's power. Trigonometric calculations are perfect examples of resource intensive computations, especially when working with embedded systems that have far more limited resources than a computer.

With the theory in mind, let's now take a look at how we can initialize lookup tables and take advantage of their power.

Application

The first step we need to take in the table initialization process is pre-calculating the cosine lookup table. The goal here is to build a precision system where we can call cos(x) and gain all of x's values. However, keep in mind that the values inside an array are of a limited size, and therefore if we want to pre-fetch them we need to calculate the finite number of values. This means that we will not be able to have cos(x) results for the total number of float values, but only for the ones that were calculated.

Let's work on an Arduino code example where we take the precision as a 0.5 degree angle:

```
float cosLookup [(int) ( 360.0  * 1 / 0.5)] ;

const float DEG2RAD = 180 / PI ;

const fl0at cosPrecision = 0.5;

cons tint cosPeriod = (int) (360.0 * 1 / cosPrecision) ;

void setup ()

{

        initCosLUT();

}
void loop()

{

        //empty for the moment

}
void initCosLUT

        for (int i = 0 ; i < cosPeriod ; i++)

        {

        cosLookup[i] = (float) cos (i * DEG2RAD * cosPrecision) ;
```

```
    }
}
```

We declared cosLookup as a float array that has a specific size. We are using 260 * 1 / precision as the number of components that are needed inside the array. In our example we have a precision of 0.5 degrees, which we can make even simpler with the following line:

float cosLookup [720]

We also added a constant in order to be able to convert the degrees into radians (DEG2RAD), and then we introduced the cosPrecision and cosPeriod so that the calculations are executed only once. Next up, we have the initCosLUT function that is used to make the pre-calculation within the setup function. Inside of it there's a loop that pre-calculates the value of cosine(x) for every x value that is between 0 and 2π. During the initialization process, the lookup table values are determined and further calculation is provided by an array index operation.

Our next step is to replace any pure calculation with array index operations. Let's retrieve the cosine values by accessing the lookup table using the following function:

float myFastCos (float angle) {

    return cosLookup [(int) (angle * 1 / cosPrecision) % cosPeriod] ;

}

We establish the angle by taking the precision of the lookup table into consideration. A modulo operation is used with the cosPeriod value in order to cover the values of any higher angles to the limit of the lookup table. This is how we have the index and therefore return the array value based on it.

Time

Since we're working with embedded software, being able to play with time is always interesting. In this section we are going to discuss the time functions provided by the Arduino core library and how we can perform some optimization operations. There's even an extremely precise function that is capable of achieving an 8 microsecond resolution.

Arduino's board chip provides us with "uptime" which represents the time from the moment the board was started. What does that mean? The board needs to stay powered up if we want to store a time and date.

Now let's discuss the main function, which is "millis." What does it do? It simply returns how many milliseconds have passed since the board was turned on. Keep in mind that according to the documentation, the number will be reset once 50 days pass. This is referred to as time overflow. Now let's create a program which measures and prints the uptime to the serial monitor once every 250 milliseconds.

unsigned long measuredTime;

void setup(){

Serial.begin(9600);

```
}
void loop(){
Serial.print("Time: ");
measuredTime = millis();
Serial.println(measuredTime);
delay(250);
}
```

The code is quite self-explanatory, even for a beginner. As a side note, this is a great demonstration why code readability matters and every programmer should focus time to practice it. With that being said, let's now ask ourselves how we can optimize this program. Naturally, this is a tiny program that doesn't truly need optimization, however we can avoid using the variable "measuredTime" and simplify it ever so slightly. Here's what the optimized version would look like:

```
void setup(){
Serial.begin(9600);
}
void loop(){
Serial.print("Time: ");
Serial.println(millis());
delay(250);
}
```

Every bit of simplicity makes your program more readable, easier to debug, and less vulnerable to errors and unnecessary resource drains. Simplicity is beautiful, don't forget that.

Next up, we can optimize our program in a different way by increasing its precision with the "micros" function. The uptime can have a precision of 8 microseconds, however the time overflow will be around 70 minutes instead of 50 days. In other words, we need to sacrifice time overflow in exchange for precision. Here's how it's done in code:

void setup(){

Serial.begin(9600);

}

void loop(){

Serial.print(«Time in ms: «);

Serial.println(millis());

Serial.print(«Time in µs: «);

Serial.println(micros());

delay(250);

}

Now that you know more about code optimization, even for the smallest Arduino projects, we can start exploring practical applications where objects can communicate with each other and react to you based on your actions.

CHAPTER 2: DIGITAL INPUTS

As you may already know the Arduino boards have a number of inputs and outputs, which provide headers that directly connect to the ATMega chipset legs. An input or an output can be wired directly to any component without requiring soldering techniques, thus making the Arduino a lot easier to work with and less messy.

Just in case you need a reminder, the Arduino has both analog and digital inputs, while the digital outputs can be forced to imitate the analog ones. In this chapter we are going to focus on digital inputs and the ability to sense the outside world. We will also discuss "Processing," which is an open source IDE and graphical library that allows you to visualize your operations graphically. Finally, we are going to experiment with switches and design a communication protocol between software and hardware.

Perceiving the Outside World

While we are currently living in a highly digitized world, not everything relies on sensors in order to perform various actions or reactions. However, humans rely on biological sensors like skin that detect temperature changes, eyes that react to light, ears that detect air movements, and a nose and mouth that process chemical compounds. Basically, we have the ability to record data and provide it for perception. In a similar manner, the Arduino board can also sense the world by having the capacity to provide some data in order to perceive the world.

Sensors are physical convertors that measure and quantify a physical state that is then translated into a signal that can be processed and understood by computers, as well as people. For instance, we used a thermometer that relies on a substance that contracts or dilates in order to give us readable data on the present temperature. The Arduino can sense in the same manner using a connected sensor. In the beginner's guide for the Arduino, we briefly discussed working with analog sensors using an analog to digital converter.

Here we are going to focus on digital sensors that can quantify any environmental conditions such as temperature, pressure, humidity, electromagnetism, light, wind speed, motion, and so on. The list is nearly endless, as there are a variety of digital sensors you can work with and all of them provide some kind of data from a measurement. While humans detect and quantify temperature by sensing it through the skin, digital sensors rely on a conversion system similar to thermometers. Thermometers rely on a volume that depends on the temperature. The height that the liquid inside it reaches is converted to a certain number of Celsius, Fahrenheit, or Kelvin degrees. This is what is known as a double conversion, and the sensors operate just like the thermometer, by integrating mathematical calculations to provide us with the data we need. However, the data that is provided by the sensor needs to be read by our Arduino board. If we use a digital thermal sensor, we first need to power it up, but we also need to measure the power potential that is generated from the pins, otherwise we wouldn't be able to perceive the temperature value.

In other words, the Arduino needs to convert this power potential into something we can read and understand. This is a basic conversion that needs to be translated and explained so that we can perceive it. But what about computers?

Computers rule over the digital domain, which is exactly the opposite of the analog domain. Everything that is analog is related to a physical measure, and the Arduino provides us with an analog input, but no output. To further understand the concept you should think about the input as a collection of reading pins, and the output as a collection of writing pins. The Arduino essentially reads what the world offers and then writes back to the world. A digital pin is set to provide us with the ability to read the power potential and convert to 0 or 1 (we will elaborate on this with switches). Now let's illustrate the theory with the help of Processing.

Processing

As mentioned earlier, Processing is an IDE and a programming language (sort of) that you can use for graphical representations. It is essentially a framework that is used to perform programming tasks through visual feedback, instead of actual programming that can be extremely abstract. Processing is the blank sheet of paper on which you can write or draw without relying on too much programming knowledge. However, we can't truly call it a programming language on its own, as it relies on a subset of Java and a number of external libraries.

Processing relies on the Java language but offers visual programming and a simplified syntax. The compilation process is also simplified, as it works just like the Arduino IDE. Now let's set it up by first downloading from processing.org/download/. Keep in mind that this framework doesn't need to be installed in the typical sense. All you need to do is place it on your computer, depending on your operating system, and simply run it. Once you start it up, you will be greeted by the Processing IDE which may seem very similar to the Arduino one. As a fun fact, you should know that you can call Processing Arduino's father, since the Arduino IDE has been taken from Processing.

Now, if you go to Files > Examples Basics you can find demonstrations for array objects and everything you need. Processing offers you everything you need to easily code, compile, and run. Now let's try out the following code and see why Processing is fun to use whether you are at a beginner, intermediate, or advanced level.

int particlesNumber = 80;

float[] positionsX = new float[particlesNumber]; // storing the particles

X-coordinates float[] positionsY = new float[particlesNumber]; // particles Y-coordinates

float[] radii = new float[particlesNumber];

float[] easings = new float[particlesNumber];

void setup() {

size(600, 600); // the size of the environment

noStroke(); // the shape we draw will have no stroke

// loop initializing easings & radii for all particles

```
    for (int i=0 ; i < particlesNumber ; i++)
    {
    easings[i] = 0.04 * i / particlesNumber;
    radii[i] = 30 * i / particlesNumber;
    }
}
// draw is run infinitely
void draw() {
background(34); // our environment's background color
float targetX = mouseX;
float targetY = mouseY;
for (int i=0 ; i < particlesNumber ; i++)
{
float dx = targetX - positionsX[i];
if (abs(dx) > 1) { // if distance > 1, update position positionsX[i] += dx * easings[i];
}
float dy = targetY - positionsY[i];
if (abs(dy) > 1) {
positionsY[i] += dy * easings[i];
}
```

```
// changing the color
fill(255 * i / particlesNumber);
// drawing the i particle
ellipse(positionsX[i], positionsY[i], radii[i], radii[i]);
}
}
```

Now run this block of Java code and move your mouse around the environment. Processing will show you a fun graphical visualization of a series of particles that follow every movement of the mouse. Keep in mind that while so far you worked with C programming, you should be able to easily understand Java, as this language derives from C. Now let's talk more about the code.

We have three important code sections. In the first part we declare all the variables and definitions. Then we have the setup function that is only run on startup, and lastly we have the draw function that runs forever until you tell it to stop. As you can see, all of these functions play a similar role, both in Processing as well as Arduino. That's because we are using the same design pattern with both tools. We begin by initiating a variable to store the particles, and then we introduce a number of arrays for every single particle we create. This design pattern is commonly used with Processing because of how readable and functional it is.

Processing and Arduino go hand in hand as they both are well-developed with a massive community built around them, open source, and available for all computer operating systems. This means that anyone can use both technologies no matter their current skill level. Many choose to work with Processing because of how easy it is to use when it comes to data visualization. Illustrating complex information with the help of basic graphical shapes can provide more insight than raw, abstract data can.

In the next section, you will learn how to combine the functionality of Processing with Arduino by building a simple communication protocol.

Linking the Physical to the Virtual

In this section, we are going to use Arduino for what it was meant to do, and link the physical to the virtual by creating a communication protocol between hardware and software. Before we begin work on our project, you should refresh your knowledge on switches.

Switches are simple hardware components that interrupt an electrical circuit. While there are several types of switches, we are only interested in two of them. One is the toggle, and the second is called a momentary, or push for action. The switches you are most familiar with are the toggles, because nearly everything you use involves one of them. The toggle works by pushing it when you want a certain action to be performed, and then release it without breaking that action. The momentary, on the other hand, needs to be continuously pushed in order for the action to occur.

Now for our project, you will have to take your knowledge from the previous book, and apply it in order to build a circuit. You will need a breadboard, wires, and we are going to use a momentary switch. First we're going to connect the ground and the +5 V of the Arduino to the top rails of the breadboard, and then use a few other rails to wire the board. There's no need to get entangled in unnecessarily long wires. Next, we will use a resistor between pin 2 and ground. The momentary switch goes between pin 2 and the +5 V line. We are going to use pin 2 as an input.

Now that we have the simple part down, let's talk about that resistor. The digital pin that we prepared to be an input is capable of sinking current, which essentially means that it works as if it was connected to ground. Provided that we have adequate firmware, we can check the digital pin and make sure it provides us with a readable value. In our example, we should be able to translate an electrical potential of 5V as a high value, and a close to 0V electrical potential as a low value. What can happen in this scenario is input signal noise that can be falsely read as an action. Because of this risk, we need to use a resistor, namely a pull-down resistor. This high impedance resistor allows a current sink to pin 2, therefore reducing any risks when operating at a close to 0 value. Both high and low values will be far more accurately detected with this type of resistor, however keep in mind that the energy requirement will be increased.

Now that the hardware is prepared, the next step is all about code. So what are the coding steps? First, we need to define the pins, as well as a variable for the state of the switch. Next, we need to set the LED pin and the switch pin as outputs, and then set up an infinite loop which will read and store the state of the input. In other words, the LED turns on if the input state is set to high, else it's turned off. Now let's see all of this in real code:

```
const int switchPin = 2;
const int ledPin = 13;
int switchState = 0;
state
void setup() {
pinMode(ledPin, OUTPUT);
pinMode(switchPin, INPUT);
}
void loop(){
switchState = digitalRead(switchPin);
if (switchState == HIGH) {
digitalWrite(ledPin, HIGH); //turn on LED
}
else {
digitalWrite(ledPin, LOW); // turn off LED
}
}
```

Now that we have that board ready with the right coding behind it, let's connect the two sections of our project with the power of Processing. We are going to use this tool to graphically display our manipulation of the switch. This phase requires the implementation of a serial communication protocol between Processing and Arduino, and we are going to design it only with the Arduino core.

As you may already know, a communication protocol is simply a rule set that is designed to guide the exchange of information between two parties, whether it's between a human and a computer or several computers. Here are the basic guidelines we need to follow when creating any basic communication protocol, including this one:

1. The protocol needs to be open to expansion in case we want to add new types of information that can be communicated.

2. Data transit is crucial, therefore we want our protocol to be able to transfer a good amount of information in a short amount of time

3. The last guideline is valid for everything you develop and it should always be on your mind. The code for the protocol needs to be readable and easy to understand by any outsider who may decide to try out your project.

Now let's discuss the design. We are going to have a two byte message that contains the switch state and the switch number. This type of message is the basic data packet you encounter in the real world extremely often. Next, we need to decide what we want to achieve. Let's say we want a circle that changes color depending on the state of the switch. If it's a dark color the switch is released, and if it's green then it's pressed. In order to write this in code, we first need to define and instantiate a serial port, followed by defining the current color to be dark. Next we need an infinite loop which will verify the receival of the serial port and the data. If this data tells the program that the state of the switch is off, the color goes from green to dark, otherwise the color will be green.

Now before we write the code, we need to use one of Processing's many integrated libraries. For our design to work, we need the serial library. To import it, you need to go to the Sketch tab, followed by Import Library and select "serial." That's it! Let's write the code:

```
import processing.serial.*;

Serial theSerialPort;

int[] serialBytesArray = new int[2]; //store the current message inside array

int switchState;

int switchID;

int bytesCount = 0;

boolean init = false;

int fillColor = 40;

void setup(){

//define the graphical environment

size(500,500);

background(70);

noStroke();
```

```
println(Serial.list());
String thePortName = Serial.list()[0];
theSerialPort = new Serial(this, thePortName, 9600);
}
void draw(){
fill(fillColor);
ellipse(width/2, height/2, 230, 230);
}
void serialEvent(Serial myPort) {
int inByte = myPort.read();
if (init == false) {
if (inByte == 'Z') {
myPort.clear();
init = true;
myPort.write('Z');
}
}
else {
serialBytesArray[bytesCount] = inByte;
bytesCount++;
```

```
if (bytesCount > 1 ) {
switchID = serialBytesArray[0];
switchState = serialBytesArray[1];
switch
println(switchID + "\t" + switchState);
if (switchState == 0) fillColor = 40;
else fillColor = 255;
myPort.write('Z');
bytesCount = 0;
}
}
}
```

Now let's discuss the process behind the implementation. We first need to create a Processing Serial Library object and a two integer sized array where we store our two byte messages from the Arduino. Next, we have a switch state and a switch ID which need to be stored in such a way to correspond to the messages we receive. The switch ID is only necessary because our design has expandability as an option, and this way we can tell the difference between multiple switches if we ever add them. Then we define init to false in the starting phase, but it switches to true once a byte is received from the Arduino.

In the second section of the implementation we define the actual environment of our graphical representation. We choose the colors, the size, and so on. Next up, we retrieve information on how many serial ports we have access to. This information is simply for debug purposes. This is all done inside the setup function which runs only once.

The third section is all about the draw function, which is quite simple. We have a fill color variable that is attached to a fill function where we instruct the program how to choose the different color and draw the circle. The circle is drawn using the ellipse function where we need to specify the x and y coordinates of the center, as well as the width and height. You may have noticed that the width and height have been chosen to be the same as the dimensions of the environment itself. This is because at some point you might want to resize the environment, and this way the circle is resized along with it with no further modifications to the code.

Finally, we have the serialEvent callback method. We use it in order to be more efficient instead of being forced to count every single time a serial port checks whether there's some data to read. We use myPort.read() to read the bytes we receive and perform the verification with the init variable. We need to see if the communication has already been established by checking whether we are dealing with the first message. If init tests as false and if the message that we receive from the Arduino is Z, then our program will clear a serial port and store information on the beginning of the communication. When this happens, the Z message is sent back to the Arduino as a response.

If communications have started, the bytes are stored into the serial bytes array and increment bytesCount. As long as we keep receiving bytes, and the count is smaller or equal to one, we concluded that the message is not whole, since it needs to be two bytes in size. Once we have the byte count equal to two, we have a whole message which we can divide into two variables, namely the switch ID and the switch state.

You can apply this approach to connecting multiple switches to the Arduino. In principle, nothing really changes and you already have the knowledge to achieve this step. With that being said, there is one more aspect regarding switches that needs to be clarified.

The Debounce Concept

In order to understand this concept, we need to peek at a microscopic level inside the switch. What is a switch and how is it made? Simply put, a switch is made out of bits and pieces of plastic and metal where we have a cap that is pressed to move a piece of metal which in turn connects to another piece of metal and thus closes the circuit. At this point, if we accurately measure the electric potential of the Arduino's digital pin, we will notice some noise that occurs approximately 1 ms after pressing the switch. This noise may seem insignificant, however it can lead to a lot of problems in any program that involves a switch.

So what happens when you press the button? There's a large chance that the counts will not be precise. For instance, if you press it once, the program might detect three or four actions. Or perhaps you pressed it four times, but only one press was registered. Any of these scenarios can occur and cause a lot of frustration. This is what we call bounce, and it has to do with the physical action of pressing the button. Keep in mind that typically when you press any button, the connection isn't fully achieved instantly. The signal may connect and break several times during the action, and this is what causes issues. It's not a defect or a design problem. It's simply how switches work.

Bouncing occurs within fractions of a second and you don't even notice it. However, the problem is that a microcontroller does notice it and detects it as more than one button press. This is why a program might detect one switch press as two or three. Bouncing leads to unwanted state changes. So how can this be fixed? Debouncing code is the answer.

There are two separate elements over which we have some control, and they are the circuit and the firmware. We can modify the circuit physically by adding capacitors, diodes, and various trigger inverters until we find the perfect balance, however this method is rather inconvenient and time consuming. This is why we are going to focus on resolving this issue through code. We are going to implement a filter based on time. Let's go through the code and see how it's done:

```
const int switchPin = 2;

const int ledPin = 13;

int switchState = 0;

int lastSwitchState= LOW;

long lastDebounceTime = 0;
```

```
long debounceDelay = 50;
void setup() {
pinMode(ledPin, OUTPUT);
pinMode(switchPin, INPUT);
}
void loop(){
int readInput = digitalRead(switchPin);
if (readInput != lastSwitchState){
lastDebounceTime = millis();
}
if ( (millis() - lastDebounceTime) > debounceDelay ){
switchState = readInput;
}
lastSwitchState = readInput;
if (switchState == HIGH)
{
digitalWrite(ledPin, HIGH);
}
else
{
```

digitalWrite(ledPin, LOW);

}

}

Our implementation of the debouncing concept can be broken down into several steps. We define a variable that is used to store the last read state, a variable that stores the time when the last debounce happened, and a delay variable. We use the millis function we discussed earlier as the time metric. Next, we have the loop cycle during which we read the input without storing it inside the switch state variable. We use this variable without changing it outside of the debounce process. Once we read the input during every cycle, we store it as a readInput variable, which we compare afterwards to the last switch state. If these variables are different, it means that some kind of change is happening, but it can either be a button press or simply a bounce. If it's an unwanted bounce, all we have to do is reset the counter. Lastly, we perform a check to compare the time since the last debounce and the delay. If it is concluded that it is larger than the delay, the cycle's last read input will be considered as the true switch state and it will be stored inside the proper variable. On the other hand, if the time since the last debounce is shorter than the delay, we will store the last read value inside the last switch state variable in order to perform a comparison check during the next cycle.

This implementation is a general one when it comes to software-based debouncing and it is used in many scenarios that involve switches and inputs corrupted by noise. In other words, anything that involves a human user can benefit from a debouncer. However, keep in mind that if we're working with system communications, debouncing won't accomplish anything. The only reason this concept is useful in the first scenario is because of the slow interactivity between user and system. Systems communicate between each other so fast that the period of time which is considered to be a real press is virtually non-existent.

CHAPTER 3: SERIAL COMMUNICATION

So far we can summarize the use of the Arduino to sharing and communicating signals. If we take it apart we can conclude that every component belonging to this device can in some way be prepared to react to a real world action and communicate data on it, whether to other components, computers, or humans.

In this chapter we are going to specifically focus on serial communication and the serial protocol. You might already know that this type of communication is used for computer to human interaction, however it is not limited only to that. Serial communication is also useful for devices to allow their own components to communicate with each other.

Are you still somewhat confused? What if you realized that serial communication is used in nearly every technology that you use on a daily basis? You may have heard of USB (of course you have), which stands for universal serial bus. This system represents a serial communication bus that is used by many higher level protocols. To lift the cloud even further, you should understand that serial communication is simply a way of sending information bit by bit through a communication bus. With that being said, let's discuss some general aspects of this concept.

General Aspects

When we discuss serial communication, we also have to include parallel communication, which is in fact its opposite. What's the difference? Let's assume we need to send eight bits of data from the speaker to the listener. If we are using serial communication, the bits will be transmitted one after another through the same channel. However, if we are using parallel communication, the eight bits will be sent at the same time through eight different channels. No matter the distance or the circumstances, serial communication will manage to outperform the parallel form, even though you might think it's slower. Sending all eight bits of data simultaneously isn't the best solution for the following reasons:

1. Parallel communication requires the same number of connections, or wires, as the number of bits of data that need to be sent to the listener. This can result in resource intensive communication, especially when our alternative, the serial communication, requires only one single wire.

2. Serial communication is simply faster. There used to be a time when this wasn't true, and parallel communication was indeed faster because of the ability to send all data simultaneously, however that is no longer the case. This is due to the fact that it is easier to handle propagation time with fewer connections, there is less crosstalk to deal with than in the case of parallel communication, and we simply save resources by dealing with a smaller number of wires.

Because of these reasons, nowadays we are mostly dealing with serial communication, whether it's done through physical wires or wireless systems. This also means that there are a great number of serial protocols to be used in this communication form.

Serial Communication Types

Serial communication becomes a bit more complicated when you take a closer look at it. It can be defined in several ways, and each one holds different characteristics. With that being said, let's briefly discuss the most common types of serial communication and characteristics:

1. Synchronous serial communication: This communication form has a timer that maintains a time reference for everyone who takes part in the communication. A simple example of the synchronous serial communication is the phone.

2. Asynchronous serial communication: There is no need for information from the timer or clock to be sent through the channel. This leads to a more efficient method of communication, however there may be problems with the ability to understand the data that passes through. For instance, texting is the perfect example of asynchronous communication.

3. Duplex mode: This is a characteristic belonging to any communication channel. It can be unidirectional, bidirectional, or bidirectional simultaneously. Unidirectional is quite self-explanatory, as the data travels only in one direction between point A and point B. Bidirectional only goes in one direction at the same time, while the simultaneous bidirectional goes both ways.

4. Peering and bus: If we have a peering system, it means that all the speakers are connected to the listeners in some way. The link can either be physical or logical.

This system doesn't require a master, and usually it is asynchronous. If we have a bus system, however, everything is linked physically.

5. Masters and slaves: As you may know, when dealing with a master/slave bus structure, we simply have a master device which is connected to a number of devices which are the slaves. This system is normally synchronous, as there is a timer inside the master.

No matter the serial communication system, the main issue you will have to deal with is avoiding misunderstandings and overlaps. Luckily, there are multiple techniques that will help you fix these problems.

One of the most important things to keep in mind when working with serial communication protocols is that you need to define the word length in bits, an empty time frame, and an error detecting solution. For instance, how can you as a listener figure out when a certain word begins if we don't define these properties? These behaviors are crucial and need to be encoded into all communication participants, otherwise the communication protocol will be invalid.

Multiple Serial Protocols

In this section we are going to discuss several serial protocols and interfaces to help you better understand serial communication. Some of them have been used in the early days of computers, and many of them are still used today.

1. The telegraphy protocol: Ever heard of Morse code? Of course you have! The Morse code telegraphy protocol is an example of one of the very first serial protocols to ever be used in communications. As you may know, the way it works is by sending either short or long signals that are separated by an empty time frame. A communications operator would transmit anything from simple words, to complex data. The protocol was implemented in a system that involves only wires that transmit electrical pulses, as well as an electromagnetic wave carrier system. This type of communication can be categorized inside an asynchronous, peering or duplex system, however there are some particular rules that need to be followed. For instance, the pulse can either be long, short, or void, however there is no timer between the two parties.

2. RS 232: This nearly 60 year old interface is still used today in many devices, especially personal computers. It is used to define the hardware used to establish connections, such as pins. The RS 232 is a point to point interface that is capable of sending data over shorter distances with great speed. Keep in mind that the speed depends on the length of the cable, as well as the type of the wire (shielded or unshielded).

3. From the 25 pin connector to 3 pins: We discussed earlier that we require a communication system capable of hardware flow control as well as error detection. The standard 25 pin connector has been used for a long time for many purposes because it offers just that, however, we can reduce its functionality to three pins. All that is needed is

a wire for data transmission, for data receival, and the ground. Keep in mind that the 25 pin connector has been designed to work with many types of devices, and this is why there is such a large number of signals going through it. For example, we have pins 8 and 22 that are meant for the phone line. In this system, we have pin 7 as the ground, pin 2 as the data transmission wire, and pin 3 as the data receiving wire. This is all we need in order to establish proper communication. This three pin communication structure is something that the Arduino also replicates within its own system. In other words, the Arduino also uses a three-wire serial interface. Both the Arduino Uno and Leonardo provide you with the same three wires.

4. The I2C multi-master bus: This system uses only a serial data line and a serial clock line, therefore in order to use it we have to start with the Arduino as the master and create the two wire bus. To know which wire goes where, you will have to check with Arduino's wire reference page which you can find on their website. The reason why this system is a great option for many projects is because data integrity is well maintained during the communication, and you have control over both short range communication as well as intermittent communication, all in the same system.

5. The synchronous serial peripheral interface: Also known as SPI for short, this interface has been designed by Motorola and includes four pins. There's a serial clock controlled by the master device, a master output and slave input, a master input and slave output, and slave

selection. The SPI is particularly useful in projects where we have a single master and a single slave. While other options can also be used in this case, this interface provides us with far more speed than an I2C system for example. This is why it is often used to provide communication between a coder or decoder and a digital signal processor. The connection involves communicating data in and out simultaneously. Keep in mind that SPI can also be used together with I2C for certain applications.

6. The USB: The universal serial bus is known to everyone, as no computer, laptop, or any electronic device for that matter can "live" without one nowadays. Why is it so popular? Simply because it offers a plug and play capability where other devices require you to restart your computer or perform some kind of setup. The USB was created to solve the communication problem between devices by offering a standardized connection for any kind of hardware. For instance, you can establish a large variety of connections such as audio, printer, webcam, flash drive, wireless, keyboard, etc.

Now that you know more about serial communication and how data is communicated inside the electronic components, we are going to build up on this knowledge in the next chapter, where we will discuss more about Arduino outputs.

CHAPTER 4: VISUAL OUTPUT FEEDBACK

When it comes to feedback, we obviously require interaction, as we are the ones performing various actions in a system, which in turn gives us the feedback required by us to perform other actions or modifications. Without feedback, we lack the necessary information needed to make certain adjustments to an application. So far we've mostly discussed working with the Arduino and manipulating its functions in order to achieve a specific goal. For example, in a previous chapter we communicated information to the Arduino with the use of switches and instructed it to perform a task.

An example of feedback can be found in an earlier chapter where we discuss the visualization of an action that occurs after a button press. This graphical representation of the result is in fact feedback. With that in mind, in this chapter we are going to discuss more about the development of graphical feedback systems. We are going to mainly use LED driven feedback deriving from the Arduino board. We will start by using some simple monochromatic LEDs, and advance towards LED matrices and multiplex LEDs. Finally, we are going to also have a brief introduction to LCD displays.

Using LEDs

As you already know, there are many types of LEDs such as the basic ones, OLEDs, AMOLEDs, and FOLEDs. When we refer to basic LEDs we are talking about the simple components that form an easy to take a part structure. OLEDs, for instance, are organic LEDs that include the layering of an organic semiconductor, while AMOLEDs are active matrix OLEDs that are used in large displays because they provide a densely packed number of pixels to render a quality image. For the purposes of this section, we are going to stick to the basic LEDs because there is no need to be concerned with added components. In the end, the principle is the same.

LEDs generally come in two shapes. You have the old fashioned ones with two legs sticking out, and the more modern versions that are wide surfaces with many connectors. These types of LEDs can be further broken down into monochromatic and polychromatic ones. In the case of polychromatic ones, you should take into consideration how easy it is to control which color is being powered.

In the following example, we are going to work with several LEDs, meaning several buttons as well. We already discussed using multiple switches earlier, therefore we can use that information in this scenario as well. Let's start by using the same circuit structure as earlier, but simply remove a switch and connect two LEDs in its place. As we already discussed, you can use the digital pins either as inputs or outputs. We are going to have two switches on one side connected to the 5V pin, and on the other side they will be connected to pin 2 and pin 3. We will also have a pull down type resistor connected to both 2 and 3 pins because we need to sink the current into the ground pin. Once these connections are established, you need to connect one LED to pin 8 and one to pin 9 and then ground both of them. Now before we get to the coding part, we need to discuss something known as coupling. This concept is important for any interaction design.

Coupling

You will find the information in this section to be useful in many interface designs meant for the communication between man and computer. As you should already know, the Arduino connects the control as well as the feedback sections together. This means that no matter what external force operates on the device, Arduino thinks of it as human. This is what is referred to as control-feedback coupling. It is a concept that contains a number of rules that define how the system interacts with the user and how it reacts when it sends us any kind of feedback. Let's say you would like to use the Arduino to exert your control over another system. In this case, you will have to perform the coupling outside of the Arduino.

With that being said, let's prepare a little program that includes coupling. Here are the two things we want to achieve with this exercise. By pressing the first switch, the first LED is turned on, and if the switch is released, the LED is turned off. We want the same thing to happen with a second LED. Now, in order to control some of these elements, we are going to use the "Bounce" library, which contains the tools we need to perform debouncing on the inputs. We already discussed this concept in an earlier chapter, therefore you should keep in mind that switch press needs to be smoothed out in order to filter any faulty button press detections. Now let's take a look at the following code and discuss it:

#include <Bounce.h>

#define BUTTON01 2   // the first button pin

#define BUTTON02 3   // the second button pin

```
#define LED01 8     // the first button pin
#define LED02 9     // the second button pin
//we will have two debouncers with a debouncing time of 7 ms
Bounce bouncer_button01 = Bounce (BUTTON01, 7);
Bounce bouncer_button02 = Bounce (BUTTON02, 7);
void setup() {
pinMode(BUTTON01, INPUT); // pin 2 input setup
pinMode(BUTTON02, INPUT); // pin 3 input setup
pinMode(LED01, OUTPUT);   // pin 8 output setup
pinMode(LED02, OUTPUT);   // pin 9 output setup
}
void loop(){
// our debouncers need to be updated
bouncer_button01.update();
bouncer_button02.update();
// debounced button states
int button01_state = bouncer_button01.read();
int button02_state = bouncer_button02.read();
// testing button states
if ( button01_state == HIGH ) digitalWrite(LED01, HIGH);
```

else digitalWrite(LED01, LOW);

    if (button02_state == HIGH) digitalWrite(LED02, HIGH);

else digitalWrite(LED02, LOW);

}

As you can see, we started by including the Bounce library in the header and by defining the constants that contain our LEDs and switches. Then we instantiate the debouncers and declare a 7ms debounce time. We have chosen this value because it is enough to make the system ignore any bouncing results. Next up, we have the setup section as usual, and we declare the button's digital pins as inputs, and the LED's digital pins as outputs. As you should recall, digital pins can be either an output or an input. In the next steps, we begin a loop where we update the debouncers and record each one's value. Finally, we take control over the LEDs and instruct them how to behave depending on the state of the switches. Now the question is, where is coupling involved in all of this? This is the true last step, as the control represented by the pressed switches is coupled to the feedback represented by the LEDs.

So far we managed to successfully connect multiple LEDs (2) to the Arduino, which means that in theory we can connect as many as we want. However, what if we're using an Arduino Uno? How can we handle more than, let's say, 6 switches and 6 LEDs to match them? The answer to this question is multiplexing. Keep in mind that this concept can also be used in the case of the Arduino Mega, in case you need to connect more than, let's say, fifty LEDs and switches to it. With that being said, let's discuss how we can effectively connect a large number of LEDs and switches.

Multiplexing

The concept of multiplexing allows us to connect a large number of peripherals to the Arduino board without requiring an equally large number of inputs and outputs. In other words, we will need only a few pins to connect many external components to the board. The connection between the peripherals and the Arduino is performed with a multiplexer and demultiplexer.

To demonstrate the concept, we are going to work with an 8 bit serial-in and serial or parallel-out component. What does that mean? The control is managed through a serial interface by using the three Arduino pins, but also uses eight of its own pins. Now let's see how we can connect 8 LED lights by using only 3 pins. We are going to connect the component to a shift register first in order to multiplex 8 outputs. With that in mind, let's take a look at the actual wiring. The Arduino supplies the power for the breadboard, while the shift register uses the ground and the 5V as its power supply and configuration. In order for the Arduino to use a serial protocol and control the shift register, the component needs to be linked to pin 11, 12, and 14. Let's examine the shift register up close. In this example we are using the 74HC595 chip:

1. We have pin 8 and pin 16 that we need for the power supply.

2. Pin 10 has to be connected to the ground so that we can activate it.

3. Pin 13 also needs to be connected to the ground, as it has to be active at all times in order to drive the device's output current.

4. Next we have pin 11 as the clock input for the shift register, pin 12 as the clock input for the storage register, pin 14 as the serial input, and pins 1 to 7 as well as pin 15 as our output pins.

In our example we are relying on pins 11, 12, and 14 for the control in order to load eight bits. The bits can then be sent serially to the device and be stored inside its register. This is what a shift register is, essentially. We simply shift bits from zero to seven as we load them.

With that being said, let's take a look at the programming side of the project. We need to use a specific design that works for this type of device. That means that for our shift register model, we need to create firmware that is specifically intended to work only with it alone. However, if we plan to use another model, the code will only require some minor modifications that are easy to make.

Now let's discuss the general design of the firmware. The first step we need to take is defining the three pins of the shift register. All three of them need to be setup as an output. This is done inside the familiar setup() section. This is how this step would look in any case similar to what we are doing:

digitalWrite(latch-pin, LOW)

shiftOut(data-pin, clock-pin, MSBFIRST, my_states)

digitalWrite(latch-pin, HIGH)

Keep in mind that this design pattern is frequently used in may shift registering operations, and you will encounter it in many other examples. Keep in mind that the storage register clock input pin (12) is what provides us with the ability to communicate with the circuit that we are going to send information through that will later be applied to the outputs. To clarify, if pin 12 is determined to have a LOW value, we are going to instruct the system to store the data we are sending. However, if it's HIGH, the data that was sent will have to go to the outputs. Next, we also need a "shiftOut" function, which will allow us to send the data to a certain pin at a certain speed in a certain transmission order. These transmission orders can either be MSB (most significant bit), or LSB (least significant bit). Before we continue, you need to first understand what these concepts mean.

Let's assume we have a byte 1 0 1 0 0 1 1 0. The most significant bit is the one at the extreme left position and having the highest value. In our example, the value would be 1. The least significant bit, on the other hand, is at the right most position and with the smallest value. In our example, the value would be 0. If we use the shift out function under these conditions, we can provide specific arguments regarding the transmission. We can either follow the MSB concept and send bits 1, followed by 0 and then 1 0 0 1 1 0, or follow the LSB concept and send bits 0 1 1 0 0 1 0 1.

Using Random Seeds

Now that you know more about the design pattern, let's discuss how we can develop a system that can generate random bytes. The bytes will be transmitted to the shift register and our array of eight LEDs will therefore have a random state. But what does random mean?

As you may already know, when it comes to computers, when we refer to random we aren't talking about something truly random. For instance, you might know about the random function, but you should also know that it is in fact a pseudo random number generator. Its more accurate name is the deterministic random bit generator, as the sequence of numbers is determined by certain established values where the seed is included. Keep in mind that numbers are generated in the same sequence for each seed. However, we have some power to influence this aspect by either forcing the seed to vary or by adding some form of randomness from an external source.

With that in mind, there is always some form or another of electronic noise interfering even if there are no wired connections. Being aware of this gives us the ability to use noise by reading the input 0. As you may already know from the previous book's analog section, we have an analogRead function which provides us with a number between 0 and 1023. We can use this in the application and define a counter variable and a byte. We can read the value that comes to the pin inside the setup method and then generate a random byte together with a bitWrite function and a loop. Then we can write every single bit of the byte by using the generated numbers from a random number function that gives us either 0 or 1 as a random result. Next, the pseudo random generated byte can be used within the same structured, however we need to redefine every seed's loop execution by reading the analog to digital conversion for pin 0.

So far we've discussed how much it would benefit us to use shift registers, as they only require a very small number of digital pins. But the question remains: what do we do if we need even more pins for a larger project? A shift register only needs three pins to power eight LEDs, but we are still limited by how many shift registers we connect. After all, we don't have an infinite number of pins to play with. The answer to this problem is daisy chaining!

Daisy Chaining

Daisy chaining is a system of wiring that is often used when we have to connect a certain number of devices together in a sequence. In this section, we are going to discuss how to use the daisy chain concept on a group of shift registers that are linked together by using the ShiftOutX library. This library can be downloaded for free from the Arduino playground section from the following link:

https://playground.arduino.cc/Main/ShiftOutX/

Now let's talk about the design. The first thing to keep in mind is that we need to communicate the serial clock, the latch, and the data throughout the chain. Serial communication needs to be synchronized with the serial clock and to instruct the shift registers that the received information needs to be stored. Any serial information that we receive from the Arduino needs to go to our first shift register, which in turn sends this data to the next one. Basically, this is how daisy chaining works.

With that being said, let's see this concept in action by examining the following code:

```
#include <ShiftOutX.h>

#include <ShiftPinNo.h>

int CLOCK_595 = 4;   // linking the first clock pin to pin 4

int LATCH_595 = 3;   // linking the first latch pin to pin 3

int DATA_595 = 2;    // linking the first serial data input pin to pin 2

int SR_Number = 2;   // declaring how many shift registers we have in the daisy chain

// enable the shiftOutX library

shiftOutX    regGroupOne(LATCH_595,    DATA_595, CLOCK_595, MSBFIRST, SR_ Number);

// our random variables

int counter = 0;

byte LED0to7_states = B00000000 ;

byte LED8to15_states = B00000000 ;

void setup() {

// there's no need to individually prepare every single digital pin as earlier

// the library takes care of everything for us

// but we need to use a seed that comes from the noise of the analog to digital conversion

randomSeed(analogRead(0)) ;
```

```
}
void loop(){
// generating two random bytes
for (int i = 0 ; i < 8 ; i++)
{
bitWrite(LED0to7_states, i, random(2));
bitWrite(LED8to15_states, i, random(2));
}
unsigned long int data;
data = LED0to7_states | (LED8to15_states << 8); // aggregate the random bytes
shiftOut_16(DATA_595, CLOCK_595, MSBFIRST, data);   // send data to shift registers
// after every 5000 loop we need a new seed for the random function
if (counter < 5000) counter++;
else
{
randomSeed(analogRead(0));    // reading new values from pin 0
counter = 0; // this is a counter reset
}
```

```
// time delay before changing the LED state
delay(45);
}
```

As you may have noticed, one of the biggest differences in our firmware pattern is the way we wrote the setup section. We no longer have to declare certain arguments for our digital pins, as the new library takes care of this part automatically. However, keep in mind that earlier in the code we have passed three Arduino pins as arguments, which actually sets them up as outputs as well.

Next, we have the usual loop section which is very similar to our previous iterations. However, we are generating two random bites in this case because we need 16 values in order to set up the shiftOut_16 function which communicates all of the data in one single argument. Generating bytes and then aggregating them into an integer with the help of bitwise operators is quite a common, standard practice, however you may have had little experience with it so far, so let's discuss how it all works.

Imagine you have the following sets of 8 bits:

0 1 1 1 0 1 0 0

1 1 0 1 0 0 0 1

Now, how do we proceed in order to store them in the same location? As already discussed, we need to start by shifting one of the bits and then add it to the next one, like so:

0 1 1 1 0 1 0 0 << 8 = 0 1 1 1 0 1 0 0 0 0 0 0 0 0 0 0

But what if we perform an extra set, and use the | bitwise operator? Here's what happens:

0 1 1 1 0 1 0 0 0 0 0 0 0 0 0 0 | 1 1 0 1 0 0 0 1 = 0 1 1 1 0 1 0 0 1 1 0 1 0 0 0 1

What we have is basically a concatenation, and this is what we achieved in our code, followed by the use of the shiftOut_16 function that transmits the data to the 2 shift registers we defined in the beginning. However, at this point you might be wondering what we would do if we'd be dealing with 4 shift registers instead. The principle remains essentially the same, but we would have to increase the shift by first using << 32, then << 16, and finally << 8 so that we can store all of the bytes into a single variable. Once the process is complete, we would have a shiftOut_32 function to communicate the result.

Keep in mind that with the ShiftOutX library there can be two groups of 8 shift registers each, which means that you use as little as 4 pins to drive 128 outputs. This makes it possible for you to rely on just a single Arduino board, however you still need to consider the amount of current. If we scale our example and use 128 LED lights, all connected to the same Arduino, and we turn all of them on at the same time, we might completely ruin the board due to the amount of current. With that in mind, most devices would just reset or shut down before burning out, but in any case you don't want to try this out on your own.

An Arduino board with a USB power supply can only rely on 500 mA without encountering serious issues. Keep in mind that the total number of pins put together can only drive 200 mA, while an individual pin can handle 40 mA at best. Naturally, these figures will vary depending on the model of the board. So far in our examples we did not have to take the possibility of a short into consideration, because we used such a small amount of power to work with a limited number of devices. However, at your current skill level you may find yourself tempted to work on a bigger project that involves more juice. Let's say your LED light requires approximately 10 mA to function properly. This means that if you have an array of 8 LEDs, you will need 80mA to power everything up simultaneously with the help of a shift register. Keep in mind that if you use more shift registers, the power requirement goes up. Another factor that is often not taken into consideration is the power requirement of your integrated circuits, such as the shift register circuit or a resistor. They consume some power but it is usually negligible. However, it might be important to take it all into account if you drive your Arduino board to the limit.

Using LCDs

In this section we are going to have a brief discussion about working with Liquid Crystal Displays. This type of technology is used in nearly everything nowadays, including in watches, monitors, phones, cameras, and so on.

There are two major types of LCDs. One is based on using a character matrix and is referred to as a character LCD, and the second is based on a pixel matrix and therefore is referred to as a graphical LCD. But how do you get your hands on either of them without breaking the budget? These days you can find circuit boards with an LCD already attached to it pretty much anywhere and it won't cost you much. In most cases, you will also be lucky enough to find one with all the connectors you need to link the device to the Arduino.

The Arduino also contains a library called LiquidCrystal, and it can be used with any type of LCD. Keep in mind that the only limitation is the Hitachi HD33780 driver that is necessary, however it is extremely common and you shouldn't have to worry about it. This dedicated driver was developed to include a micro controller that makes it possible for character LCDs to connect to the outside world with the help of a 16 pin connector. With that being said, let's play around with an LCD and display some random messages with the following lines of code:

```
#include <LiquidCrystal.h>

String manyMessages[4]; int counter = 0;

// initializing the library with the number of pins in the circuit

LiquidCrystal lcd(12, 11, 5, 4, 3, 2);

void setup() {

// LCD columns and rows

lcd.begin(16, 2);

manyMessages[0] = "My name is Arduino";

manyMessages[1] = "I have the ability to communicate!";

manyMessages[2] = "My sensors help me feel things!";

manyMessages[3] = "I am even able to react!";

// roll the dice

randomSeed(analogRead(0); }
```

```
void loop() {
// set the cursor to column 0 and row 0  lcd.setCursor(0, 0);
// 5s each
if (millis() - counter > 5000)
{
lcd.clear(); // clear the whole LCD
lcd.print(manyMessages[random(4)]); // displaying a random message
counter = millis();
}
// set the cursor to column 0 and row 1
lcd.setCursor(0, 1);
// print the value of millis() at each loop() execution
lcd.print("up since: " + millis() + "ms");
}
```

As usual, the first step we need to take is implementing the LiquidCrystal library into our firmware. Next, we have two variables, namely an array of strings that is needed for the message storage, and a counter that we need for time tracking. The library is then initialized and the variables are passed in such a way to fit with every pin that is required to wire an LCD to our Arduino. Keep in mind that the order of the pins is very important in this process, therefore you should go with rs, enable, d4, d5, d6, and d7. Inside the setup section, we need to use the hardware information in order to define the dimensions of the LCD. In our example we define it 16 columns and 2 rows. The next step is to store a number of messages inside the array, and then use the loop section to place our cursor on the first position of our display. In this block of code, we also check whether the following operation is true: (millis() – counter > 5000). If it is, then we can clear the entire display and then print a random message. Take note that we create a pseudo randomly generated number between zero and three, and because we are using a random index the display message will be chosen randomly from the ones we defined. Lastly, the present time is recorded in order to have a time measurement that tells us how much time passed since the previous message was displayed. The cursor is then placed on the second row, first column, and a string is printed. This string contains information on the variable that displays how much time passed since the Arduino was reset.

CHAPTER 5: MOVEMENT

So far we focused on data communication and sensors, however the Arduino can also react to movement. Whether we are talking about objects moving, or producing air movements (sound), this little board is up to the task.

In this chapter, we are going to discuss taking control of servo motors and learn how to take advantage of using transistors to manage higher amounts of current. We will also explore the area of sound generation. As the main project for this chapter, we are going to develop a synthesizer that can be controlled through MIDI. Let's get to work!

Using a Piezoelectric Sensor

One of the best ways to illustrate Arduino's versatile capabilities is to introduce you to the piezoelectric sensor, which allows us to design an object that moves with the help of the firmware we design. So far we focused on visual feedback, however keep in mind that there are other types of feedback that can be useful in many scenarios such as this one. For instance, let's say we are attaching some devices and piezoelectric sensors to a jacket. Visual LED feedback wouldn't be useful for this project, however we can send feedback to the person wearing the jacket by using vibrations. With these sensors on either side of the jacket, we can send feedback in different forms depending on what kind of interaction the wearer is performing.

The piezoelectric sensor is a device that relies on the piezoelectric effect, as the name suggests. This effect can be defined as a linear electromechanical communication between an electrical state and a mechanical state in certain objects. In other words, the mechanical action generates the electricity and therefore it can be used for vibration or movement detection. However, if we supply the power to the object, it vibrates and therefore it is perfect for our little project. We essentially use the sensor as a way to generate vibrations. On a side note, because of these characteristics, the piezoelectric sensor is frequently used as a tone generator, however we're going to save this fact for later when we are going to discuss more about sound in particular.

In case you are worried about power consumption, a piezoelectric sensor rarely needs more than 15 mA, which your Arduino can easily deal with. However, in case of a more complex project, you should always check the official document behind the device you are using in order to make accurate calculations. In our project, we are going to use a generic piezoelectric sensor that has only two legs and is connected to the Arduino through a digital pin capable of pulse width modulation, or PWM. In case you don't recall, the reason why we are relying on PWM is because for this project we need to mimic an analog output current by using digital means. The general idea is to use the analogWrite function in order to feed the sensor with different voltages. With that being said, let's take a look at our code for generating vibrations and discuss the technical side of the project.

```
int piezoPin = 9;

int value = 0;  // storing the value of the feed

int incdec = 1;  // storing the variation's direction
```

```
void setup() {

}
void loop() {
//checking the value of the current and changing the variation's direction if needed
if (value == 0 || value == 255) incdec *= -1;
analogWrite(piezoPin, value + incdec);
delay(30);
}
```

As you can see, the analogWrite function fulfills the purpose of taking the digital pin as a value, as well as an argument. The value goes from 0 to 255 and it takes the place of an analog output by mimicking it. We use the function with the increment / decrement parameter in order to store an increment value for every single loop that is carried out. This value will change whenever it reaches one of its limits, whether it's 0 or 255, and then it inverts itself. This is a simple method of forcing the cycle to keep going from 0 to 255 and then the other way around, without requiring any resource intensive operations. Basically, this code controls the sensor by making it vibrate from a lower, less intensive value to a higher setting.

Now that we covered a simple movement control example, let's proceed with a more advanced project where we discuss how to manipulate larger, more complex motors.

Transistors

Before we move on to more complicated motors, we need to take a side step and discuss more about transistors. So far in previous chapters we have mentioned them, and used them as digital switches. Keep in mind that they are incredibly versatile, and therefore can be used as a way to stabilize voltages or in place of amplifiers. Because of their frequent use, you can find these little devices everywhere and you won't have to break the bank to acquire them.

In case you need a reminder, a typical transistor has three legs, namely the base, an emitter, and a collector. Now, if we flood the base of the transistor by attaching a power supply to it, with 5 V worth of current, all of the power that comes from the collector will be sent through the emitter. This makes the transistor an excellent device for controlling the large amount of energy that the Arduino cannot drive on its own. Keep in mind that when the transistor is used in this manner, the Arduino can control it simply because such a tiny power supply is required by the base of the transistor.

Understanding this design pattern is important for the projects we are going to discuss, as well as for many projects you might pursue on your own in the future. Keep in mind that having an external power supply is often needed, and recommended, when working with motors. With that being said, let's apply what we discussed to the practical application of servo motors.

Using Servomotors

As you probably already know, a servomotor is characterized by a rotary actuator that provides us with the ability to fine tune an angular position. Servos are widely used in many technologies and nowadays can be found at a very low cost pretty much everywhere. When purchasing one for your robotics projects, you should keep in mind that not all of them are equal, meaning that some require a great deal of power. Why is this important in our case? We are working with an Arduino, and powerful servomotors require a stronger supply than the board can provide. In translation, you would only be able to use one servo or two at most, unless you use an external power supply.

When do we use servomotors? Whenever your project demands the ability to control an object's position based on its rotation angle. Servomotors aren't needed only for making various components turn or rotate inside your robot. They can also be used to move the entire object. This is how most Arduino robot projects are built, and you can find many examples of them if you do a quick search. For instance, a servomotor would often be attached to the arm or leg of a machine where another component will be attached from the other side of the device. Imagine the servo as a joint that offers mobility. So how do we take care of the technical aspect of working with servomotors?

Luckily, Arduino provides us with an extensive library that contains everything we could possibly need. This library is appropriately called Servo, and it allows us to use a maximum number of 12 servomotors on typical Arduino boards, and up to 48 if we're using a Mega board. For now we are going to presume that we have access only to a simple board in order to work out what kind of design limitations we have to face. An example of such a limitation is the fact that pins 9 and 10 won't work with the analogWrite method we used earlier.

Keep in mind that most servomotors come in a 3 pin package containing the ground, pulse, and 5V. Basically, we have the control pin, however the pulse will be the board and as a power supply we are going to use an external source such as a battery. With that being said, let's take a look at the code behind the design of an application that provides us with cyclical movement between 0 and 180 degrees.

```
#include <Servo.h>

Servo myServo;

int angle = 0;  // current angle

void setup() {

myServo  myServo.attach(9);

}

void loop() {

for(angle = 0; angle < 180; angle += 1)

{

myServo.write(angle);

delay(20);

}

for(angle = 180; angle >= 1; angle -=1)
```

```
{
myServo.write(angle);
delay(20);
}
}
```

As always, we start by including the required library and by instantiating the object, in this example being myServo. Inside the setup section we first need to connect the servo object to pin 9 and therefore define the pin as the control for myServo. Next up, we have the loop section where we declare 2 "for" loops in the same fashion as previously done in our piezoelectric sensor example. A cycle is defined where the angle is incremented progressively from 0 to 180 degrees and then decremented backwards. We also added a 20 ms delay in-between the cycles. Lastly, we have the Servo.read function which reads the present angle of the device. This operation is required in case we want to perform some dynamic changes without storing the values every single time.

Multiple Servomotors

Now that you know the basics behind working with one servomotor, let's discuss what it takes to use more of them simultaneously. For most projects there isn't much you can do with one motor, therefore you should know the intricacies behind operating multiple ones.

With that being said, let's consider using three motors. As already mentioned, servomotors simply perform the operation of converting power to movement, therefore the more of them we use, the more current we need to manage. Provided you are using your Arduino connected to a PC, the power supply provided through the USB connection is only enough as long as you don't go over 500 mA. For anything more than that, you need an external power source. This means that when using three servomotors or more, you will need to use either a power supply adapter connected to your wall socket or batteries. In this example we are going to use the classic AA batteries. Don't forget that you can always use batteries to simply power your board and thus gain some freedom of movement without being forced to be connected to a stationary computer.

Keep in mind that when using batteries in this way, we have to wire all of our grounds together. We can do this simply because the batteries will be our only power supply for the motors and nothing else. Now let's dive straight into the code and see how we can control the three servomotors:

```
#include <Servo.h>

Servo servo01;

Servo servo02;

Servo servo03;

int angle;

void setup() {

servo01.attach(9);
```

```
servo02.attach(10);
servo03.attach(11);
}
void loop()
{
for(angle = 0; angle < 180; angle += 1)
{
servo01.write(angle);
servo02.write(135-angle/2);
servo03.write(180-angle);
delay(15);
}
}
```

The code is quite self-explanatory, and you shouldn't have trouble understanding it. The servomotors are instantiated and every one of them is connected to its own pin inside the setup section. Then we have the loop block, where we handle the angles by defining an angle variable. As in earlier examples, the variables goes into a repeating cycle from 0 to 180 degrees, and the motor that is connected to pin 9 is driven with the value obtained from the variable. The second motor that is connected to pin 10, however, is driven with a value that goes from 135 to 45 degrees.

The third motor is then driven with an angle value of 180 degrees, which as you may notice is the opposite movement of the first motor.

The firmware we wrote is the perfect example of how to control a single variable, while also being able to build variations around it. In our example we have varied angle values and we also create different variable combinations depending on the expression. Now, keep in mind that this isn't the only approach you can take to solve the problem on using multiple servos. We can also control the motor's position with the help of an outside parameter. For instance, we can use the measured distance or the potentiometer's position. With that being said, we are going to extend some of these concepts in the next section where we are going to discuss stepper motors.

Stepper Motors

Sometimes called step motors, these devices can be controlled through small steps, as the name suggests. The rotation of the motor is split in equal steps, therefore the position of the motor can be held at any of these steps. This is done accurately and without the need of any kind of feedback system. The control over the movement is asserted either forward or backward by manipulating the step sequence. The Arduino is extremely capable of handling the entire process, and that is why stepper motors are a great addition to your project toolkit. With that being said, let's discuss in more detail the unipolar stepper motors.

Also referred to as unipolar steppers, these motors are built using a central shaft and 4 electromagnetic coils. The reason they are called unipolar is because they only use the current that comes through a single pole. Keep in mind that in a similar way to the servomotors, it is recommended that you control the stepper motor with an external power supply. The best option in this case, however, is to use the wall adapter instead of AA batteries. All you need to do is take pins 5 and 6 and send some power through them. The next step you need to take is using the board to control pins 1, 2, 3, and 4 with the help of a Darlington transistor array such as the ULN 2004 or ULN 2003 devices. In case you don't know, a Darlington array is used to achieve high power amplification by boosting the current from the first transistor with the second transistor and so on. In our case the ULN2004 would be better suited because it can handle up to 15 V of power, while the ULN2003 is at 5V only.

When working with a stepper motor, we need to have control over extremely accurate movements, and in order to achieve this we need to know certain sequences which can be found only in the device's datasheet. The sequences table would look something like this one:

Step	A	B	C	D
1	HIGH	HIGH	LOW	LOW
2	LOW	HIGH	HIGH	LOW
3	LOW	LOW	HIGH	HIGH
4	HIGH	LOW	LOW	HIGH

The idea is that if we plan to perform a rotation clockwise, we need a sequence going from step 1 to 4 and back to 1 again. This is done cyclically over and over again. If you need to perform a counterclockwise rotation, you simply need to generate the opposite sequence. But how do we handle all of this through code without writing a large number of sequences? Luckily, there's a function for that inside the adequately named Stepper library which is part of the Arduino. With that being said, let's take a look at the following code:

```
#include <Stepper.h>

#define STEPS 200

// we need a stepper instance

Stepper stepper(STEPS, 8, 9, 10, 11);

int counter = 0; // storing the number of steps that occurred since the last direction shift

int multiplier = 1;

void setup() {

stepper.setSpeed(30); // 30 RPM speed

}

void loop() {

// random movement from at least one step

stepper.step(multiplier);

// count the number of steps that were moved
```

// reset the counter and switch direction once an entire turn is reached

if (counter < STEPS) counter++ ;

else {

counter = 0;

multiplier *= -1;

}

}

Once we prepare the Stepper library, we have to define how many steps are there in one rotation. If we take a look in the stepper's datasheet, we will see that the first step is represented by a 1.8 degree angle and with only a 5% margin of error. Keep in mind that this value will differ based on the model of your stepper motor, so make sure to check and change the value accordingly. Now, because the error is so small, we can consider it as a negligible factor and ignore it entirely. Therefore, we only take the 1.8 degree value into consideration. Knowing this number, we can calculate how many steps we need in order to perform a full rotation. The answer is 200 steps, as 200 * 1.8 = 360. The next step is to instantiate the stepper object with 5 specific arguments, the four Arduino pins that are connected to the device, and the step value needed for a full rotation. Before we continue, we also need a variable that handles the rotation change, and another that handles the tracing.

Next up, we have the setup section where we define the speed that actually drives the motor. We declared a value of 30 rounds per minute, which can always be modified inside the loop section if the circumstances change for various reasons. In the loop block, we push the motor to a value that is equal to a multiplier which for starters is set to 1. In other words, whenever the loop method is executed, the motor will rotate from the 1.8 degrees step clockwise. When we perform the test, we check for every round of completed steps that translate to a full rotation. As soon as we determine that we've reached rotation limit, the counter is reset and the multiplier is inverted, therefore the motor can continue in the opposite direction.

What we discussed so far can be labeled as design patterns. They can be useful in a variety of situations, so make sure to take note of them as they may give you an idea for a cheap solution that is light on resources.

Sound

As already mentioned, this chapter's main focus is movement, so why are we discussing sound? Just ask yourself: what is sound if not an air movement that produces audible data? In this section, we are going to discuss this topic because the Arduino can make the air move, just as well as it can make a robot move. Keep in mind that this will not be a complete guide to sound, but you will learn the most important topics and concepts behind working with sound. This is the beauty of developing projects with an Arduino. It is an incredibly versatile device that can perform a vast number of tasks, so let's dig in!

The simplest way to think of sound is as a mechanical wave that oscillates and can pass through various materials, whether gas, liquid, or solid. We can broaden this explanation by looking at sound as the result of these transmitted waves once it hits the human ear. When you look at it this way, you can conclude that the ears are somewhat complicated sensors that detect changes in air pressure. Our "sensors" are able to detect the movement of air (sound amplitude) and the variations in the air movements (sound frequency). Now keep in mind that all of this data from these processes is transmitted and received in real time, whether we're discussing the mixture of lower sound frequencies or higher. A certain sound can include a number of various frequencies. Our perception of sound is the summary of a number of frequencies that have certain amplitude.

As you can see, we can describe sound in several ways, however there are two general representations of it that we should consider in our Arduino projects. We are either discussing an amplitude variation over a certain amount of time, which can be represented through visual methods such as graphs, or an amplitude variation that depends on what the frequency contains. With this in mind, if your project ever requires you to convert from one representation to the other, there's a mathematical operation that does just that. It is called the Fourier Transform, and it provides you with efficient and accurate calculations.

Now, let's take an example of the most basic type of sound wave, which is the sinusoidal air pressure variation. Let's first discuss the time domain representation of it, which is the amplitude variation over time we mentioned above. In this representation, we are looking at a cyclical sound variation with a period of time which is equal to the wavelength. What exactly is this period we're referring to? It represents the amount of time it takes for one oscillation cycle to be completed. In other words, if we manage to define the sound variation over a certain period of time, we can illustrate the visual representation of sound. Now, if we discuss the sound that originates from a specific source, the variation over a period of time will be the equivalent of the air pressure's variation. By creating a graphical interpretation of this process, we can observe the direction of the axis that matches the so called "high pressure front," which is a section of the curve represented by the time period axis. What this basically means is that we are dealing with a high pressure which presses against the inside of the human ear. Once this curve goes under zero, we are dealing with a pressure that is lower than the ambient pressure. The human ear will detect this difference.

On the other hand, when we are looking into the frequency domain representation, the graphical interpretation is seen as a simple vertical line. Keep in mind that in the time domain representation we have a graph with a pulse-like structure that illustrates the sound frequency. This visualization can be summarized with the following equation: $T = 1 / f$. In this formula, the time period is measured in seconds and represented by the T symbol, while f is the frequency which as you know is measured in Hertz. A higher frequency level leads to a higher pitched sound, and lower frequency leads to the opposite, which is a lower pitched sound. Another thing to keep in mind is that a higher frequency will also involve a much faster vibration performed over a short period of time.

Let's take a look at microphones and speakers for a moment. A microphone is a sensitive sensor that is capable of detecting extremely subtle changes in air pressure. This means that they work by simply translating these oscillations or vibrations into shifts in voltage. A speaker, on the other hand, has a mobile section which works in a similar way to the human ear in the sense that it can push or pull air. This results in vibrations, and therefore sound. The movement is achieved with the shifts in voltage. Both of these devices rely on a special membrane, while the microphone also has an electrical transducer which is necessary in order to perform air pressure changes that eventually translate to electrical signals. The speaker works by modifying electrical signals, and this process results in a pressure change. Keep in mind that both of these devices involve analog signals, and not digital.

We mentioned earlier a sound source, and we need to elaborate on this. You should take note that not all sound sources are the same. For instance, you register a sound by knocking on a piece of wood. This would be referred to as analog sound, because you perform a physical action that makes the material vibrate, thus causing oscillations in the air pressure around it. Those oscillations are then detected by your ear. On the other hand, we could be using some kind of digital device. This, however, leads to hardware limitations, and therefore we'll have difficulties making an analog description.

With that being said, we have covered some of the fundamentals behind sound and frequencies. It may seem like we briefly strayed from this chapter's topic, however it is important for you to understand the basic theory behind a concept before you actually pursue building an Arduino project. Now let's explore the concept of digitizing sound and then learn how to use the Arduino board to read and write audio signals.

Digitizing Sound

Let's say we have a system that samples the voltage variations that occur inside a microphone. When we discuss sampling we are referring to the technique of sampling and holding, which means that our system reads the analog data regularly during set time intervals. The value is received and then placed on hold until a new value is received. This is the sampling rate which is used to describe sampling frequency. With a low rate, the analog signal result is also lower, but if there's a high rate the signal is higher as well. Now, keep in mind that there is a limit that we need to take into consideration. This limit is referred to as the Nyquist frequency.

The sampling system requires the sampling to be performed at double the highest frequency inside the signal. This results in a higher accuracy and precision rate, however the downside is that we also end up with a much larger file that requires more storage. However, there is more to this process.

Another thing worth taking note is the bit depth. When working with digital devices, we required a bit-based system that represents the value of the amplitude. The bit depth can be defined as the outcome of the amplitude going from -1 to 1. The basic idea is that with a higher bit depth value we can record more using a digital system. With a lower bit depth the result would be a lower sound quality that simply doesn't contain a great deal of subtleties. For instance, let's say we have a bit depth of 0.5 to 0.7. In this scenario, we would lose the variation that resulted from the value in-between, which is 0.6. The result would either be 0.5 or 0.7, thus losing sound subtlety.

that both the bit depth and the sampling relies on ... them for. The final rendering determines our purpose, which in turn determines the quality standard we have to use. There are mainly two such standards. One is the CD quality at 44.1 kHz and 16-bit, and the other is DAT at 48 kHz and 16-bit. Other options include 96kHz and 24 bits, frequently used by various sound recording studios, and 16 kHz and 8 bits used by certain enthusiasts that are looking for an old fashioned sound.

With that being said, let's talk more about the process of going from analog to digital. As you may have already guessed, this is handled by the analog to digital converter that we mentioned several times in this book as well as in the previous one. Keep in mind, however, that in order to perform a proper conversion we required good quality sound from the start, otherwise the quality will suffer significantly. The entire process is handled the same way as the Arduino already does when working with an analog input. The analog to digital converter is at 10 bits and will read the value in 111 ms intervals, which translates to a sampling rate of 9 kHz. During this process several buffers are needed to smoothen everything out.

Keep in mind that this entire process can also be performed in reverse. A digital sound can be converted to an analog sound with, you guessed it, a digital to analog converter. Data is sent by the processor into the converter as a set of values, which are then transformed into an electrical signal, and therefore analog sound.

Producing Sounds with Arduino

Now that we've covered the basic concepts behind sound, we can start involving the Arduino in producing or listening to sounds. As you already know, the board can write and read both digital as well as analog signals, meaning it can also process audio signals. On top of this functionality, we can also connect various components to improve the process further. For instance, we can use an analog to digital converter or a digital to analog converter to store the sounds. Nowadays, it's common to rely on hardware to control the firmware, and this allows us to use the Arduino as a starting point to build a collection of various controls that we then interface with our computer's software. The Arduino board can also be used to trigger sound, by transforming it into a sequencer that produces MIDI messages to a connected audio synthesizer. With that being said, let's start discussing more about sound related techniques that are specific to Arduino.

As you already know, we need two components in order to play a sound, namely an audio source and a speaker. In case you aren't yet familiar with all of Arduino's subtle intricacies, you should be aware that the board can produce on its own 8 kHz / 8-bit sounds when connected to a computer's speakers. We can use the tone function that is provided by the Arduino in order to perform an operation referred to as bit banging. We have to manipulate the board's pins in such a way so they don't hinder the pulse width modulation output from pins 3 and 11 and then toggle the input and output pins at a certain frequency.

Now let's take a look at some code where we'll use sound frequencies to create some "music" instead of actual tones.

```
void setup() {
// we require a pseudo random number generator
randomSeed(analogRead(0));
}
void loop() {
// we need to generate a pitch and duration, both of them being random
int pitch = random(30,5000);
int duration = 1000 / (random(1000) + 1);
// playing a tone to pin 8
tone(8, pitch, duration);
// add a pause
delay(duration * 1.30);
// stop the sound
noTone(8);
}
```

Now let's go step by step through the code and discuss the entire process. The first step is to implement a pseudo random number generator and then generate two numbers inside the loop block. First, we have the pitch with a value between 30 and 4,999, which represents the sound frequency. Secondly, we have the sound duration which is measured with a value between 1 microsecond to 1 second. Both of these arguments are needed for our tone function to be properly implemented. Once this step is achieved, we call the function and pass the pin which feeds the speaker, as an argument. A frequency wave is then generated. At this point you need to keep in mind that the sound will continue for as long as we don't call the noTone function. This is why we need to define a certain duration. The result of this code, as mentioned, is an 8-bit "song" with pseudo randomly generated tones.

CHAPTER 6: ADVANCED TECHNIQUES

Now that we've discussed a number of new individual techniques which you can apply to your Arduino projects, we can start discussing certain concepts that can either be implemented on their own or in combination with what you've learned so far. Intermediary level, and later advanced, projects will require a great deal from you. Simple techniques will not be enough to finish a real world project, therefore you need to start learning some of the more subtle concepts that complement your work.

In this chapter we are going to explore new tools and concepts that will aid you in your future Arduino projects. You will learn how to work with components such as the electrically erasable programmable read-only memory (EEPROM for short), how to use GPS modules, and how to improve the autonomy of your board. Let's get started!

Improved Data Storage

So far we've only worked with devices that are entirely dependent on power from the Arduino in order to function as programmed. This means that once there is no more current flowing through the component, all of the data and information that we gather is lost and we need to start over. Keep in mind that this doesn't mean that your actual firmware is deleted and you need to rewrite it. So, how do we solve this problem?

Most Arduino boards have three different memory types, namely the flash memory, static RAM, and EEPROM. All of these memories have their own purpose. The firmware you code is stored inside the flash memory. When the programming takes over and reads, writes, and handles variables and functions, all of this data is stored inside the static random access memory. The electrically erasable programmable read-only memory, on the other hand, is what we need in order to store something for long periods of time. From this type of memory nothing will be deleted once you turn the board off.

With that being said, let's take a look at how we can write and read using the EEPROM library. We are going to go through some code that reads all the bytes inside the memory and then prints the results.

```
#include <EEPROM.h>

// the first byte (0) is where we start reading from the memory

int address = 0;

byte value;

void setup() {

// open port

Serial.begin(9600);

}

void loop() {

// use the present address to read a byte

value = EEPROM.read(address);
```

```
Serial.print(address);
Serial.print("\t");
Serial.print(value, DEC);
Serial.println();
// continue in order with the next address
address = address + 1;
// we have 512 bytes inside the memory
// when we reach address 512, we wrap around back to 0
if (address == 512)
address = 0;
delay(500);
}
```

Now let's go through the code line by line and understand what's happening. The first thing we do is instantiating the EEPROM library. Then we follow up with the variable definition that represents our ability to store a currently read address. This variable needs to be initialized at 0 as this is the start of the memory register. Keep in mind that the variable needs to be defined as a byte data type. Next up, we have the setup section where we need to initialize the serial communication, followed by the loop section where we store the current address. The result is then printed to a serial port. Take note that in the Serial.print("\t") line we are talking about tabulation, which means that we are writing the data in such a way to make it readable and easy to understand.

Next, we move on to the next address where we perform a verification process to see whether it is equal to 512. If the result is checked as true, the address counter is reset to 0 and the process continues until the value of 512 is reached again. In this function we also add a short delay.

Now that we've gone through the basic process, let's discuss more about external EEPROM connections. These memory storage devices are widely available on the market and they are fairly cheap. Whenever you consider that your project might benefit from relying on this type of storage, don't hesitate to purchase it due to budget restrictions. With that being said, we are going to take a look at an EEPROM model that uses I2C to perform all reading and writing operations. The 24LC256 is one such model, and it provides us with a handy amount of memory space of 32 kilobytes. If you require more memory, you can also opt for its big brother, the 24LC1025, which also relies on I2C and has a storage capability of 1024 kilobytes. Now let's take a closer look at what makes this EEPROM tick.

We have the chip address inputs labeled as A0, A1 and A2, followed by 5V connection and the ground pin. We also have write protect pin, or WP for short. This means that if we connect it to the ground, we can still write to the memory storage, however if we connect it to the 5V pin it won't work. Next up, we have two other connections that are part of the I2C communication, namely the serial data line and the serial clock line. You need to pay particular attention to these wires, as the connection will differ based on the type of your Arduino board. Always make sure to check the documentation before you proceed with making the connections. For example, the Arduino Mega2560 has the serial data line under pin 20 and the serial clock line under pin 21, while the Arduino Leonardo has them under pin 2, and pin 3, respectively.

With that in mind, let's talk about the firmware. We are going to need to work with the "Wire" library, which handles our I2C communication requirements. This library is available straight from the Arduino and it can handle raw bits, among other things. Now let's see how to use this library and then discuss the code:

```
#include <Wire.h>

void eepromWrite(byte address, byte source_addr, byte data) {

Wire.beginTransmission(address);

Wire.write(source_addr);

Wire.write(data);

Wire.endTransmission();

}

byte eepromRead(int address, int source_addr) {

Wire.beginTransmission(address);

Wire.write(source_addr);

Wire.endTransmission();

Wire.requestFrom(address, 1);

if(Wire.available())

return Wire.read();

else
```

```
return 0xFF;
}
void setup() {
Wire.begin();
Serial.begin(9600);
for(int i = 0; i < 10; i++) {
eepromWrite(B01010000, i, 'a'+i);
delay(100);
}
Serial.println("Bytes written to external EEPROM !");
}
void loop() {
for(int i = 0; i < 10; i++) {
byte val = eepromRead(B01010000, i);
Serial.print(i);
Serial.print("\t");
Serial.print(val);
Serial.print("\n");
delay(1000);
}
```

}

Once we import the library we need, we have to define the write function and the read function. Their purpose is to read and write the bytes from our external memory storage system with the help of the Wire library. The next step is to instantiate both the wire and the serial communication inside the setup section of our code and then use a "for" loop that determines how we write the information to a certain address. We specified that this information is in fact the character "a," followed by a number. What does this mean exactly? For instance, when we write the state, we can have the character "a" + 9 which results in character "j". Keep in mind that the purpose of this example is to demonstrate how easily and efficiently we can store data, even if it may not be extremely meaningful or valuable. In the next step, we print a message to the serial display which informs us that the writing process has been finished and the information is now stored inside the EEPROM. Then we have the loop section of the code where we read from the storage system.

There are a few things you need to keep in mind when working with the Wire library. Firstly, it handles two bits, namely the start bit and the acknowledge bit. Secondly, we have the chip select bits which can be modified by simply rewiring the A0, A1, and A2 pins to the ground wire, as well as the +V wire. This translates to eight different address variations that go from zero to seven. In binary they look like this: 1 0 1 0 0 0 0, 1 0 1 0 0 0 1, with the eighth address being 1 0 1 0 1 1 1. The first address is translated as 0 x 50 while the last one is translated as 0 x 57. In our example we wired the three aforementioned pins to the ground, and then the memory storage system's address becomes 0 x 50 when using the I2C bus. This doesn't mean that we have to use only one bus, however it isn't necessary unless we require a higher amount of storage space. With this information, you can now use the EEPROM's storage capacity to store anything you want, whether it's audio data, lookup tables, or simply any kind of information that requires more room than the Arduino provides you with by default.

Working with GPS Modules

In this section, we are going to focus on using modules specifically designed for projects that require the implementation of a global positioning system.

As you probably already know, GPS works by having a receiver that registers signals communicated by a minimum of four satellites. Each one of them has an atomic clock installed, which is used to calculate the propagation time of the signals and perform a precise calculation of a 3D position. As challenging as this may sound to some, it is pure trigonometry, however we are not going to dive into more mathematical details as they aren't necessary for the purpose of this section. Our goal is to parse data that originates from various GPS modules.

With that being said, let's take a look at the Parallax GPS receiver which provides the Arduino with the ability to detect a position without requiring a large amount of resources.

The Parallax GPS Receiver Module

This module provides us either with raw NMEA 01823 strings, or certain data that is requested by the user from a serial command interface. NMEA 01823 is a combination of electrical and data specifications that are required for the communication between various electronic devices such as sonars, autopilot systems, and GPS receivers. It works by using ASCII communication protocols that determine how information is transmitted from a transmitter to a listener.

With that being said, the parallax receiver module has the ability to track up to 12 satellites, as well as WAAS, which is a system that helps with the signal calculations. On a side note, WAAS is a system specific to the USA. The module itself provides us with various parameters such as the current time, date, latitude, longitude, altitude, speed, heading, and a lot more. This means that we can write data that requests certain strings from the module, however keep in mind that some of them are automatically transmitted. Here are some of these strings:

1. Global Positioning System Fix Data - $GPGGA
2. GPS satellites in view - $GPGSV
3. GPS DOP and active satellites - $GPGSA
4. Recommended minimum specific GPS data - $GPRMC

All of this data needs to be extracted by our Arduino board and then placed into application. Now let's take a brief look at the wiring behind this module. The receiver requires one single data pin, namely pin 0. At this point you might recall that we discussed earlier how we can't use the USB port for any kind of serial monitor at the same time as pins 0 and 1 are used for various serial features. Our serial implementation is full duplex when it comes to serial communication that relies on pins 0 and 1. In our example, the module would transmit data to the board through digital pin 0, which would also be connected to the USB Rx pin. Then the USB Tx pin would be used to transmit data to the computer when wired to digital pin 1. While this communication method works perfectly in our scenario, we have to also take the possibility of interferences into consideration. We do not want to transmit data from the computer to the board by using the USB. Why? Because we will encounter problems due to the fact that the USB is already busy receiving data from the module by being connected to pin 0.

When working with this module we will need to implement the serial.write function in order to write data to pin 1. Keep in mind that at this point the USB Tx pin is not connected to anything else. This means that we can transmit data to the USB without any kind of issues. Then we use the serial.read function to read from pin 0 as well as the USB. Just keep in mind that we will not transmit any kind of data from the computer to the USB. This is important in order to read from pin 0 with no risks involved. The final step we can take is pulling the /RAW pin set to low mode so that the module extracts data from the board without the user being forced to request it manually.

Parsing Data

Before we start creating our software implementation, there is one more step we need to take. We cannot take advantage of the data extracted from the GPS module without knowing what this device can transmit. In this case, you should first examine the device's datasheet in order to fully understand what you are dealing with. To make things easier for you, using the device we discussed earlier, here's an example of the type of information that we can transmit:

1. $GPRMC: this is what defines the kind of data sequence we can transmit and also includes the UTC time to fix.

2. 220516: This is the data status, which includes either a valid position or a warning.

3. A: This represents the latitude of the positional fix.

4. 5133.82: This refers to the north or south latitudes.

5. N: This is the longitude of the positional fix.

6. 00042.24: This represents the east or west longitudes.

7. W: This is the speed measured in knots.

8. 173.8: This is tracking measured in degrees.

9. 231.8: This is the UTC date of the positional fix.

10. 130694: This represents the magnetic variation and it is measured in degrees.

11. 004.2: This is the eastern or western magnetic variation.

12. W*70: This is a checksum, which is a digit that represents the sum of correct digits inside any kind of transmitted data. The purpose of this is to check for any kind of errors that may appear during the transmission process.

With information on the type of data we can transmit, now we can start coding the parser which is needed for the software component. Let's take a look at the code and then discuss it:

```cpp
int rxPin = 0;  // This is our Rx pin or pin 0
int byteGPS = -1; // Current read byte
char line[300] = ""; // Buffer
char commandGPR[7] = "$GPRMC"; // Message related string
int counter=0;
int correctness=0;
int lineCounter=0;
int index[13];
void setup() {
pinMode(rxPin, INPUT);
Serial.begin(4800);
// We need to clear the buffer
for (int i=0;i<300;i++){
line[i]=' ';
}
}
void loop() {
byteGPS = Serial.read();
```

```
// Test whether the port is clear
if (byteGPS == -1) {
delay(100);
}
// if the port isn't clear
else {
line[lineCounter] = byteGPS; // the read data goes into the buffer
lineCounter++;
            Serial.print(byteGPS);   // the read data is then printed to the serial monitor
// We need to verify that the transmission has ended
// If it's finished we start parsing the data
if (byteGPS==13){
            counter=0;
correctness=0;
// We need to check if the command we received starts with $GPR
// If it does, then the correctness counter is increased
for (int i=1;i<7;i++){
if (line[i]==commandGPR[i-1]){
correctness++;
```

```
}
}
if(correctness==6){
for (int i=0;i<300;i++){
// store position of "," separators
if (line[i]==','){
index[counter]=i;
counter++;
}
// store position of "*" separator
if (line[i]=='*'){   // ... and the "*"
index[12]=i;
counter++;
}
}
// Write data to serial monitor on the computer
Serial.println("");
Serial.println("");
Serial.println("---------------");
for (int i=0;i<12;i++){
```

```
switch(i){
case 0 :
Serial.print("Time in UTC (HhMmSs): ");
break;
case 1 :
Serial.print("Status (A=OK,V=KO): ");
break;
case 2 :
Serial.print("Latitude: ");
break;
case 3 :
Serial.print("Direction (N/S): ");
break;
case 4 :
Serial.print("Longitude: ");
break;
case 5 :
Serial.print("Direction (E/W): ");
break;
case 6 :
```

```
Serial.print("Velocity in knots: ");
break;
case 7 :
Serial.print("Heading in degrees: ");
break;
case 8 :
Serial.print("Date UTC (DdMmAa): ");
break;
case 9 :
Serial.print("Magnetic degrees: ");
break;
case 10 :
Serial.print("(E/W): ");
break;
case 11 :
Serial.print("Mode: ");
break;
case 12 :
Serial.print("Checksum: ");
break;
```

```
}
for (int j=index[i];j<(index[i+1]-1);j++){
Serial.print(line[j+1]);
}
Serial.println("");
}
Serial.println("---------------");
}
// Reset the buffer
lineCounter=0;
for (int i=0;i<300;i++){
line[i]=' ';
}
}
}
}
```

At this point you might feel a bit confused, but don't worry, we're going to discuss every operation we performed with this code. Let's first "decipher" the variables because we have quite a few of them. Here they are:

1. rxPin: This variable represents the digital input to which the module is connected. Also known as digital pin 0.

2. byteGPS: This variable is simply the most current byte read that comes from the device. Keep in mind we are using serial communication.

3. line: This is our buffer array.

4. commandGPR: We need to parse messages, and this is a string variable that does precisely that.

5. counter: This is simply the index of the index array.

6. correctness: This variable is used to store the validity of the messages.

7. lineCounter: We need this variable in order to keep track of the data's buffer position.

8. index: This variable stores the position of GPS's string separators.

Now that we've gotten that out of the way, let's start discussing the firmware in more detail. As always, we have a setup block where we define the Rx pin (pin 0) as our input, in order to begin the serial communication. The communication is performed at a rate of 4800 baud. If you take a look at the parallax receiver's datasheet, you will see that this rate is a requirement for the serial interface. On a side note, baud is a measurement unit used in telecommunications, as well as electronics, and it represents the speed of the communication over a certain data channel. Always examine your datasheet to make sure you follow all of your device's requirements, otherwise the code won't work as desired. The last part of the setup section also includes a clearing of the line array buffer. This operation is performed by simply filling the buffer with a space character.

Next, we have our usual loop section where we start by reading the byte from digital pin 0. Keep in mind that if the port contains something, we skip to the else block. However, if the port is empty, we simply wait for a period of 100ms before attempting to read it again. The parsing process starts by placing the data inside the buffer at the index of the lineCounter array. Once this operation is underway we need to start incrementing the index in order to properly store any data we receive. The read data is then printed in a raw line to the USB port, allowing us to display it as raw data to the serial monitor. Once we have the data, we verify it by comparing it to 13 and testing it to see whether the communication is complete and the parsing process can start. The counter and the correctness are then reset, and we perform a test to see if the first six characters stored inside the buffer are equal to $GPRMC. Whenever we obtain a match, the correctness variable is incremented.

Keep in mind that this is a standard pattern and you will make use of it in other scenarios as well. If all of our data checks turn out to be true, the correctness variable is equal to six and this in turn means that our tests are correct. This process assures us that we are using the correct NMEA $GPRMC sequence and therefore we can parse the data. Once we divide the string by storing the position of every single comma separator, we perform the same process for the "*" symbol. We need to tell the difference between the characters and determine in which section of the message they belong. This is why we also use a number of switch / case statements. We need them to be able to print the correct messages that contain the GPS data we are looking for. Lastly, we finish the project with a "for" loop where we begin with the j index by using the array index at a certain position.

Based on the position of each separator, we start progressively incrementing every single value. This allows us to basically parse and use location data as necessary with the help of our module. At this point, we can use this information for a variety of purposes and create a number of projects. For instance, we can combine the data with visualization techniques and create a program which records your location. We can store this data every 10 seconds on the EEPROM we discussed earlier and then use it to create a graphical representation of it.

During this section you may have been asking yourself what the point of this project is when we don't have the ability to move around with the Arduino in our pocket. This is a power related problem, as we obviously require enough energy to power both the Arduino as well as the GPS module, while also being able to walk on the street with it. This is where we start discussing the problem of autonomy. Let's see what we can do to make the board mobile and usable in a lot more scenarios.

Arduino Autonomy

To refresh your memory, the Arduino can be powered in two different ways. We either connect it to a computer via a USB cable, or we use an external power source, such as batteries. So far, we relied mostly on working with a USB power supply because it's the easiest and most practical way to build a project. However, in cases such as our GPS project example, mobility is essential and without it, the project becomes nearly useless. Now, keep in mind that the board rarely requires more than 50mA worth of power, however, in most cases you will have a certain number of external devices and circuits connected to it.

We've already seen in an earlier example how quickly a set of LED lights can add up to that power requirement.

This doesn't mean that you should immediately give up on using a USB power supply, however. There are projects that simply cannot function without a connection to a computer via the USB cable. For instance, for data communication purposes this type of connection is mandatory and you can't go around it. With that being said, this is in fact the main reason we need a USB connection. Another issue we need to consider is the amount of power our project consumes, because the board can only handle up to 500mA through the USB port. If we go beyond that amount we risk serious damage to the hardware.

With that being said, if you're considering external power sources, there are two kinds you can opt for. You either go with batteries or a power adapter. We briefly used both methods in previous projects, but now is the time to expand on both of these power sources so that you can decide how your project can benefit the most.

Using Batteries

As you may recall, both the Arduino Uno as well as Arduino Mega can function by using an external power source ranging from 6 V to 20 V. However, the standard practice for optimal use is to use power supply with a range between 7 V and 12 V instead. 9 V is considered by many to be the ideal amount of voltage. Now, before we connect an external power supply to the Arduino, we need to handle the power jumper. This means that our first step is to place the jumper on the board's external power supply side which is labeled with EXT. This step is valid for a number of boards, however make sure to read up on your model because some of them are slightly different.

Now let's connect the power supply to the board with some simple wiring. All you need to do is grab a standard 9 V battery and connect its positive terminal to the Arduino's VIN pin and the negative terminal to the GND pin. Keep in mind that while the 9V battery is recommended due to the VIN pin's 12V limit, you can also opt for a 12V battery. If you choose to take this route, make sure that the battery doesn't supply you with a current value higher than 500 mA.

That's it! The power supply is connected, and now the battery will feed the Arduino and any external devices connected to it with enough power. But what if the 9V or 12V battery is too big and too heavy for your project? Not a problem. There are other types of batteries you can go with. For instance, we have the coin-sized cell batteries that can supply you with enough power while weighing as much as a feather. With this type of battery, however, you will need to purchase a cell battery holder in order to properly connect it to the board. Another limitation to keep in mind is the fact that a regular cell battery can supply you with 3.6 V and 110 mAh, and this might not be enough to power your project if you are working with an Arduino Uno, for instance. In this case, you may have to consider using an Arduino Pro Mini instead, as it requires only 3.3 V to operate.

When we're talking about power supply alternatives, you should also consider using the Arduino Pro Mini, as it doesn't require a large power source and it can also be embedded into other systems. The board is small and can easily be hidden inside walls, or plastic containers that fit inside your pocket. It is an excellent tool that provides you with all the mobility you could possibly need. If you choose to go with mini, however, you also have the option of using polymer lithium ion batteries, as they are perfect for autonomous devices.

Now, the question remains: what if we require a lot more power than batteries can provide us with? The answer is power adaptors!

Using Power Adaptors

Sometimes we have too many devices connected to the board for batteries to suffice. This is when we have to rely on an external power supply that isn't as limited and can also provide us with the mobility we need. Luckily, power adapters are readily available and an Arduino adapter is easy to come by. Just keep in mind that if you opt for an off the shelf adapter, you need to make sure that it is a DC adapter with an output voltage between 9 V and 12 V. You also need to guarantee a minimum of 250 mA current, or better yet 500 mA. Keep in mind that when it comes to power adapters you don't have to limit yourself to 500 mA, you can go even for 1 A. Finally, you need to make sure that the adapter comes with a center positive 2.1 mm power plug.

Once you make sure that your power adapter is with the center of the connector as the positive part, you need to start considering the voltage and current features. Examine the product information that comes with your adapter and check for labels such as OUTPUT: 12 VDC 1 A. You can also go with the 5 A version of that same adapter. Keep in mind that the current is supplied only by what you already have in your circuit. If you purchase a power adapter that releases a higher current, the circuit will not be damaged simply because it will only receive as much current as it needs. This is why there are a great number of adapters out there that can be used with the Arduino.

Always remember that when working with power adapters, you will have to calculate the current inside the circuit. This is where Ohm's law comes back into play, as we discussed it in an earlier chapter. You will have to consult the datasheet of a certain component in order to check how much current goes through it. Let's take an RGB LED for instance. The forward current may be around 20 mA with the possibility of hitting 30 mA at its peak use. This means that if we are connecting 5 such LEDs and enabling them to use the maximum amount of power to achieve the highest brightness, we will have to perform the following calculation: $5 * (20 + 20 + 20) = 300$ mA. The three values come from the fact that RGB LEDs need to light up the red, blue, and green. This result would refer to the normal use of these LEDs, however the peak would be around 450 mA. At this point the lights are turned on at their maximum potential. Don't forget that a common strategy to reduce the power when working with LEDs is to turn them all in quick succession and not simultaneously. This reduces the amount of power they require and your project could benefit from more LEDs without the extra power.

We won't dig deeper into the mathematical calculations, but you should always consider the basic rules of electricity whenever you are attempting to perform an accurate calculation of your energy consumption. At this point you might want to consider using an Ampere meter or voltmeter. The voltmeter is used to measure the voltage that is running between point A and point

B, while the Ampere meter measures the current between certain points across your circuit. However, even if you are using these tools, you should consider making the calculations as well and pay attention in order not to override the board's pin capacity, or the USB 450 mA limit.

CHAPTER 7: NETWORKING

In this chapter we are going to discuss creating networks with multiple Arduino boards and computers, and make them communicate with each other through various network protocols. Once you learn about creating data networks, we are going to progress to building Ethernet links between the devices. This step is crucial because it will provide you with the knowledge you need to build any project that relies on the Internet. We will also explore ways of developing Bluetooth communications, as well as methods of connecting the Arduino to other computers without using cumbersome network cables. Don't forget that many projects require mobility, and connecting your board to the Internet without any wires can open up a great deal of options.

But before we get started, you should ask yourself what a network really is when you strip it down to the basics. A network can be simply described as a system of various components connected to each other. This definition encompasses a variety of networks, including electrical grids, highways, as well as data networks. Naturally, in this section, we are interested in data networks that already surround us in our daily life. We have video service networks, phone networks, global communication networks, and so on.

Open Systems Interconnection

We will focus on different kinds of networks and discuss how we can share data from different types of media. However, before we start discussing the relation between Arduino boards and network implementations, we are going to explore the Open Systems Interconnection model which was developed in the 70s. Why are going to talk about something so old? Because this model's purpose is to define the requirements around various communication systems. It is a layer focused model that basically defines which features and protocols are needed in order to develop a communication system.

When we're discussing communication protocols, we are referring to a system of rules and formats that provide the base for communication between a minimum of two parties. With every single layer we have one or multiple functionality implementations and every single entity interacts with the layer below it and provides the resources needed by the layer above it. Essentially, protocols enable objects from one host to interact with the equivalent objects from another host, but inside the same layer. One host transmits data to another host, in this case known as a payload sometimes, which is then passed to the layer below. In order to retrieve this data, a header and footer are required to be added to it, depending on which protocol is used. This process is referred to as encapsulation and it goes all the way down to the bottom layer, which is the physical one. The receiver requires the flow of bits to be modulated, and the data needs to pass through the layers and communicate the flow to each one of them by using the aforementioned headers and footers. These elements are then deleted all along the layer path. This is known as decapsulation. When the data's journey is complete and the receiver receives it, it can finally process it. Keep in mind that at every level, the two hosts are communicating to each other by using the protocol data unit, or PDU for short. As a follow up, the service data unit (SDU) is also called. This type of data is passed down from one layer to another, only downwards and only to layers that haven't been encapsulated yet. Every single layer examines the received data as an element which either adds or deletes headers and footers by following the rules set by the protocol.

With that being said, let's take a look at all the layers and protocols in order to gain a better understanding.

Layers and Protocols

As mentioned earlier, in this section we are going to briefly discuss the purpose of every single layer and explore certain examples of protocols.

1. **The Physical Layer**: This is the layer that determines which physical specifications are needed in order to establish data communication. This includes pin structure, voltage, impedance, network adapters, host bus adapters and so on. The first major function this layer performs is the initialization of a connection to a communication channel. This also includes the termination of said connection. Participation in the control processes that involve shared data is another function provided by the physical layer, together with the ability to process the conversion between communicated data and the signals

which transport it. Here are some of the most popular standards that are found in this layer: Bluetooth, USB, and optic fiber networks.

2. **Data Link Layer**: This layer is in fact divided into two sections. One is the media access control, and the other is the logical link control. Both of them provide the ability to transfer the data between various network systems, as well as an error detection service. This last function looks for errors inside the previous layer and can even fix them. Here are some of the most popular standards that belong to this layer: Ethernet, Wi-Fi, and I2C.

3. **The Network Layer**: This layer allows us to transfer data in-between hosts that are located in separate networks. It provides us with routing, fragmentation, and reassembly and error reports. The routing is needed in order to give the hosts the ability to communicate with each other. Fragmentation and reassembly go hand in hand, as these functions cut or divide the data into smaller pieces for easier transmission and then reassemble them at the final destination. The router is the main component here because it needs to be connected to multiple networks in order to allow the data to travel between them.

4. **The Transport Layer**: This layer ensures the data transmission between the users, and it is located in between the network layer and the application layer. It provides us with error control, flow control, and the segmentation or desegmentation of data. The protocols related to this layer are either connection-based, or state-based, which

means that we can monitor travelling data segments and in case they fail to arrive at the destination (failed transmission), we can restart the transmission process automatically. There are two standards that you should be aware of when discussing this layer, namely TCP and UDP. As you may already know, TCP is the one that is connection-focused because it maintains the communication by making sure all transmission components are working as intended. UDP, on the other hand, is stateless and its purpose is to resend a transmission request when something goes wrong.

5. **The Application Layers**: These layers are the final step of a network transmission and therefore they are part of the OSI model. Here are some examples of client / server applications: FTP for basic file transfers, POP3 and other applications for mail services, SSH for secure shell communication, and finally HTTP for web browsing and more.

IP Addresses and Ports

Before we can start wiring the Arduino to a local area network, we need to cover some basic aspects regarding IPs and ports. Don't worry, this won't turn into a full blown course about networks and network administration. We will only stick to the bare bone requirements.

With that being said, ask yourself what exactly is an IP address? The simplest way of defining it would be as a numerical address which is referenced by any device that seeks to communicate over a certain network. Keep in mind that there are two types of IP addresses, namely IPv4 and IPv6. This is worth taking note of, because for the time being only IPv4 is relevant to us because it is the only version that is available to users. Currently IPv6 is not supported by a great number of routers and servers, therefore making such a connection could cause complications. IPv4 represents the addresses that are coded over 32 bits, while IPv6 represents the addresses with a length of 128 bits. As you already know, an IP address is written as a collection of 4 bytes that are separated by a point, thus making it easily readable. While a regular address looks something like 192.122.1.555, some of them have a more unique structure and cannot be routed through the internet.

The next question is, what is a subnet? This is a method of splitting a network into smaller fractions. As you probably noticed, a standard network configuration contains the IP address, a subnet mask, and a gateway. The IP together with the subnet mask are the elements that determine the range of the network. This is essential to obtaining information on whether a transmitter can directly communicate through the receiver via a network connection. Keep in mind that if the receiver is found inside the same network, communication is direct, however if it is on the outside (in a different network), that transmitter needs to use the gateway as an intermediary which routes the data until it reaches its destination. The gateway contains all the information it needs regarding which network it connects to. This means that it can send data to various networks, and even filter some of it if we implement some kind of rule set with specific limitations. With that being said, the subnet has a similar structure to the IP address. Here's an example of a subnet mask: 255.254.255.0.

Lastly, we have the communication port which is connected to the transport layer we discussed earlier. Let's assume we want to transmit a message to a host for a certain application. The receiver can only receive this message by being in listening mode, which means that we need an open communication port. Normally, an application is capable of opening its own port, however you should keep in mind that once it's open and used, a different application can no longer have access to it. The end result is a highly versatile and interconnected data trading system.

Another aspect to consider is that if we need to transmit data to a certain host, but for multiple applications, we need to specify that the message is meant for said host, to different ports corresponding to each application. As you might assume, this doesn't mean that we can proceed however we want. There are various standards designed for global communications and we need to adhere to the set rules. For instance, the HTTP protocol that is related to web-based data exchanges requires TCP port 80. On the other hand, we have UDP port 53 that is required for any operation involving DNS.

With that being said, you should now have enough basic knowledge to start working on your first Arduino networking project. Let's start learning how to wire the board to a wired Ethernet system.

Using Wired Ethernet

As you probably know, Ethernet refers to the local area network you are already using on a daily basis. Normally, Arduino boards do not offer you the ability to use the Ethernet, and therefore you need to use an Arduino Ethernet Shield and a 100BASE-T cable. For this project we are going to work with Arduino UNO R3. If you are planning to use a different model, please make sure to always check the device's datasheet because certain things are bound to differ from our example. With that being said, the reason we need to use these two components is the fact that they provide us with the necessary network connectivity and the aforementioned cable is much longer than your default USB cable.

The Arduino Ethernet Shield is in fact an Ethernet module that is usually sold together with a PoE device. In case you don't know, PoE stands for Power over Ethernet, and it basically is a power supply that feeds other modules through an Ethernet connection. In our example, however, we aren't going to be using the PoE.

Now let's start developing a system that uses Ethernet communication between our board and a small program. The plan is to connect the Arduino to the computer through the Ethernet. We are going to be sending a message from the board to the computer program through the UDP. Our program will react by sending messages in return, which as a result will flip an LED switch on to let us know that communication is established. For this step we are going to connect a simple switch that toggles the Arduino's default LED light. Remember that the connection to the computer is established through the Ethernet cable.

In order to provide our board with the ability to transmit messages through the Ethernet cable, and therefore the network, we need to define the specific conventions that are required by the firmware. For our programming, we will have to use the Ethernet Library because it enables us to use specifically network related functions and features. Keep in mind that this library, like the others mentioned throughout the book, is available straight from the core. Now let's take a look at the code and discuss the process in more detail afterwards:

#include <SPI.h>

#include <Ethernet.h>

#include <EthernetUdp.h>

#include <SPI.h>

#include <Ethernet.h>

#include <EthernetUdp.h>

// Defining the switch and the LED

const int switchPin = 2; // switch pin

const int ledPin = 13; // LED pin

int switchState = 0; // variable needed to store the current state of the switch

int lastSwitchState = LOW;

long lastDebounceTime = 0;

long debounceDelay = 50;

// Defining the network

```cpp
// defining the IP address, port and a MAC address for the board
byte mac[] = {
0xDE, 0xAD, 0xBE, 0xEF, 0xFE, 0xED };
IPAddress ipArduino(192, 168, 1, 123);
unsigned int ArduinoPort = 9999;
// The computer's UDP port and IP address
// We need to modify the port and the IP based on our configuration
IPAddress ipComputer(192, 168, 1, 222);
unsigned int ComputerPort = 10000;
// Send/receive buffer
char packetBuffer[UDP_TX_PACKET_MAX_SIZE]; //buffer
// Need to instantiate the Ethernet UDP instance to send and receive packets through the UDP
EthernetUDP Udp;
void setup() {
pinMode(ledPin, OUTPUT); // set the LED pin as an output
pinMode(switchPin, INPUT); // set the switch pin as an input
// starting Ethernet and UDP
Ethernet.begin(mac,ipArduino);
Udp.begin(ArduinoPort);
```

```
}
void loop(){
// if a packed is received, read it into the packet buffer
if        (Udp.parsePacket())        Udp.read(packetBuffer,UDP_TX_PACKET_MAX_SIZE);
if (packetBuffer == "Light") digitalWrite(ledPin, HIGH);
else if (packetBuffer == "Dark") digitalWrite(ledPin, LOW);
// read the state of the digital pin
int readInput = digitalRead(switchPin);
if (readInput != lastSwitchState)
{
lastDebounceTime = millis();
}
if ( (millis() - lastDebounceTime) > debounceDelay )
{
switchState = readInput;
}
lastSwitchState = readInput;
if (switchState == HIGH)
{
// send a packet to processing if the switch is pressed
```

```
Udp.beginPacket(ipComputer, ComputerPort);
Udp.write('Pushed');
Udp.endPacket();
}
else
{
// send a packet to processing if the switch is pressed
Udp.beginPacket(ipComputer, ComputerPort);
Udp.write('Released');
Udp.endPacket();
}
delay(10);
}
```

As always, we start by importing the required library, in this case being the Ethernet library. The next step is to declare all of the variables that are needed to handle the LED, switch debouncing, and network features. Once we've made the preparations, we need to start defining the shield's MAC address, which is unique to every device and can be found in the accompanying user manual or on a sticker glued to the back of the module. Keep in mind that this means you have to check your own address and type it inside the code, otherwise our little project won't work.

Once that is taken care of, we include the Arduino's IP address. In this case we need to make sure that the address can be reached. The way to make sure your computer can reach the IP is by working on one single network, or on a different network but with a router as the intermediary between the two networks. Just make sure that your IP address is unique to the local network. The next step is to choose the UPD port. This is needed to establish proper communications, and in our example we are working with network parameters that are connected to the personal computer. Then we define a buffer where we deposit the current received messages. Pay attention to the UDP_TX_PACKET_MAX_SIZE constant that we declared, as it is used to save some memory. If you check the library's documentation you will see that it is included with it. Next up, we need to instantiate our EthernetUDP object so that we can transmit and receive data through UDP.

The next section of our code is as usual the setup function, where we declare the statements for the LED, the switch, and the Ethernet. At the start of the block, we establish the Ethernet connection by using our IP and MAC addresses. Next, the UDP port is opened and defined. Then, we have the loop section, which as you can see is a little bit more complex than in our previous projects. We start by performing a verification that checks to confirm whether Arduino is receiving any packets. If a packet was registered, the parse packet function is called if the size is not zero. Keep in mind that this function is also part of the Ethernet library. Once the result is established, the data is read and then stored inside the packet buffer. The final step of this stage is to check whether the variable is equal to light or dark, which refers to the Arduino switching the LED on or off. We also perform a check to see if the switch is pressed or not, and based on the result a UDP message is transmitted.

Keep in mind that this is only the first half of our project. We still need to develop the program required to communicate as planned over the Ethernet. Let's start first with the code for this application and then discuss it in detail:

```
import hypermedia.net.*;

UDP udp; // defining our UDP object

String currentMessage;

String ip = "192.168.1.123"; // the IP address belonging to the Arduino

int port = 9999; // the UDP port belonging to the Arduino

void setup() {

size(700, 700);

noStroke();

fill(0);

udp = new UDP( this, 10000 ); // need to create a UDP socket

udp.listen( true ); // check for message

}
void draw()

{

ellipse(width/2, height/2, 230, 230);

}
void receive( byte[] data ) {
```

```
if ( data.length == 6 || data.length == 8 )
{
for (int i=0; i < data.length; i++)
{
currentMessage += data[i];
}
// if the message is equal to Pushed
// then answer with "Light"
if (currentMessage == "Pushed")
{
udp.send("Light", ip, port );
fill(255);
}
else if (currentMessage == "Released")
{
udp.send("Dark", ip, port );
fill(0);
}
}
}
```

Once we import the hypermedia library, we define the UDP object and a string type variable which holds the current received message. Keep in mind that we have to define the IP address of the Arduino here as well, just like we did in the first half of the project. We also need to define the open port which is available to the Arduino. In both blocks of code the port is 9999. As you may have guessed, all of this information needs to precisely match what we defined earlier in the board's firmware. Next, we have a setup function where we define several parameters followed by the instantiation of the UDP socket to port 10000. This UDP port is then set to listening mode because we need to wait for any incoming communication.

Next, we have the draw function where we simply define a circle. Then the receive function is used as a callback for the incoming packets. The size of the packets is measured and verified in bytes because we need only two messages. We are looking to reach a push or release, and therefore we test whether the packet length is either six or eight bytes. Every other packet that doesn't fit our definition will go ignored and unprocessed. Keep in mind that our testing system isn't perfect and there is room for improvement. We are using only a basic check and for the purpose of this exercise, it works well enough. If you want to stretch your wings, feel free to seek for ways to improve it.

The Arduino reacts accordingly whether it receives a "pushed" or "released" message. If "light" is communicated, the circle will be filled with a white color, and if "dark" is communicated, the circle will be filled with a black color. That's it! We now have a simple communication protocol that relies on the Ethernet and UDP. Now, let's broaden our networking horizon and discuss Bluetooth communications.

Using Bluetooth

Another functionality you have access to with the Arduino is Bluetooth. As you may know, this is a type of wireless tech that allows you transfer data over very short distances. The data exchange is performed using a short wavelength radio transmission. This system also permits you to create personal area networks which can be implemented on computers, phones, and other devices. Keep in mind that not all Arduino models have Bluetooth technology readily available. If you are using a common board like the Arduino Uno, you will have to purchase an external Bluetooth module.

At this point you might be feeling somewhat frustrated due to having to deal with so many external modules because the board doesn't offer them natively. You really shouldn't. From a project design perspective, it's considered better to use a basic board to which you connect only what you actually need. For instance, there's no point in working with a big board that already comes with an external power supply, a Wi-Fi module, and a Bluetooth module when all you need to achieve is lighting up one single LED. Always go with a generic board for the core of your project and add only what tools you need.

With that being said, we are going to work with the Arduino Uno, which requires a Bluetooth module to be connected to it. We are going to work on a project that requires the use of Processing. This project will involve a Processing environment where if a mouse click is detected, the application will transmit a message using the Bluetooth connection, to the board, which in turn will light up its LED to notify us that the message is received. We are going to be using the RN41 Bluetooth device in this example, so make sure you check your device's datasheet to make the appropriate connections and modifications. You will also need a computer with Bluetooth capabilities. Keep in mind that many desktops don't come with this feature, so you may have to purchase a separate Bluetooth module for your PC, or use a laptop instead. All laptops come with Bluetooth, generally. Now, let's take a look at the firmware:

```
// handling our LED
const int ledPin = 13; // the Arduino's pin connected to the LED
void setup() {
pinMode(ledPin, OUTPUT); // we need to set the LED pin as the output
Serial.begin(9600); // starting serial communication
}
void loop()
{
if (Serial.available() > 0) {
incomingByte = Serial.read();
if (incomingByte == 1) digitalWrite(ledPin, HIGH);
else if (incomingByte == 0) digitalWrite(ledPin, LOW);
}
}
```

All we had to do here is instantiate the serial communication with our Bluetooth device. We also have to perform a verification process to see whether there are any bytes coming from it and then parse them. The LED is then switched on if a message is available, or switched off if there isn't. Now let's take a look at the code for our application:

```
import processing.serial.*;

Serial port;

int bgcolor, fgcolor;

void setup() {

size(700, 700);

background(0);

stroke(255);

bgcolor = 0;

fgcolor = 255;

println(Serial.list());

port = new Serial(this, Serial.list()[2], 9600);

}

void draw() {

background(bgcolor);

stroke(fgcolor);

fill(fgcolor);
```

```
rect(100, 100, 500, 500);
}
void mousePressed() {
if (mouseX > 100 && mouseX < 600 && mouseY > 100 && mouseY < 600)
{
bgcolor = 255;
fgcolor = 0;
port.write('1');
}
}
void mouseReleased() {
bgcolor = 0;
fgcolor = 255;
port.write('0');
}
```

Now that we have the code, let's take a closer look and understand what's happening. Processing's serial number needs to be imported, as discussed in previous projects. As usual, we have the setup block of the code where we define the drawing elements and print the list of the serial device to Processing. Next, we have the draw function where we prepare our environment. We set up the background color, the stroke color, and the fill color based on self-explanatory variables. We basically draw a square and then we introduce the mouse pressed and mouse released functions to be called whenever a mouse event is registered. When the mouse button is pressed, our application verifies the position of the mouse cursor during this action. As you can see in the code, we have designated a specific area inside our environment, which is the square, and if we press the button within its confines we receive visual information. This lets us know that the information was transmitted and received, and the digital write function writes the value of 1 to the module. In a similar fashion, when we release the button, the function writes the 0 value, to let the Bluetooth module know that the mouse button was released. All of this information is transmitted to the Arduino board, which as a result will switch the LED light on or off.

That's it! We have successfully implemented an external Bluetooth module that gives us the ability to communicate over short distances. One thing worth noting at this point is that the library we used isn't generally necessary. The Bluetooth module is capable of sending and receiving data on its own without any kind of assistance. We only implement this library when we want to send serial data. However, in our example we're working with serial data between the Arduino and the module, and that is why we're using the library.

Now that we've covered the Ethernet direct connection and Bluetooth as well, let's discuss data communication over a Wi-Fi connection.

Using Wi-Fi

Now that you know more about network communications and we worked with short range Wi-Fi, we can finally explore wireless medium range communication that you will frequently use when building your own projects.

But what exactly is Wi-Fi? We can summarize this technology as a set of wireless protocols controlled by the IEEE 802.11 standards which describe the features and rules of wireless local area networks. Basically, several hosts with Wi-Fi connections, or modules, can transmit and receive information by relying on their IP stacks. Keep in mind that there are several networking modes that this type of communication uses and in each one of them hosts connect and communicate differently.

For instance, we have infrastructure mode, where the hosts use an access point for communication with each other. The hosts, as well as the access point, have to be defined using the identical service set identifier. This identifier is basically a network name that allows the hosts to use it as a reference point. One of the characteristics of this mode that sets it apart from others is that every single host has to go through the access point before gaining access to the global network. This means that security is much tighter than in other modes. There are other modes as well, such as the ad hoc mode, where the connection between hosts is direct, or bridge mode where several access points are linked to each other. However, we won't dig into these any deeper.

The main component we need to focus on is the Arduino Wi-Fi shield. This is what gives our board the ability to perform a wireless connection. It's also worth noting that this device also comes with a slot where you can insert an SD card, meaning you have increased storage capabilities as well. The shield provides you with wireless connection features, network encryption methods, serial debugging features for the module, as well as a mini USB connector so that you can update the shield's firmware.

Connecting the Wi-Fi module is a simple task, as there's no wiring involved. You simply plug in it and you feed it some code. Now we are going to connect the shield and test a simple connection using the ConnectNoEncryption example that can be found inside the WiFi library. Using the native library, we will have access to everything we need to perform a wireless connection to any network. Now let's take a look at the code and discuss the entire process:

#include <WiFi.h>

char ssid[] = "yourNetwork"; // introduce your network's name

int status = WL_IDLE_STATUS; // wifi status

void setup() {

//wait for this port to open once you initialize the serial

Serial.begin(9600);

// performing a check for the presence of the module

if (WiFi.status() == WL_NO_SHIELD) {

Serial.println("WiFi shield not present");

// don't continue

while(true)

delay(30) ;

```
}
// try to connect to the Wifi network
while ( status != WL_CONNECTED) {
Serial.print("Attempting to connect to open SSID: ");
Serial.println(ssid);
status = WiFi.begin(ssid);
// adding a 10 second delay to wait for the connection
delay(10000);
}
// print out data once the connection is established
Serial.print("You're connected to the network");
printCurrentNet();
printWifiData();
}
void loop() {
// perform a connection check in 10 second intervals
delay(10000);
printCurrentNet();
}
void printWifiData() {
```

```
// print the module's IP address
IPAddress ip = WiFi.localIP();
Serial.print("IP Address: ");
Serial.println(ip);
Serial.println(ip);
// printing MAC address:
byte mac[6];
WiFi.macAddress(mac);
Serial.print("MAC address: ");
Serial.print(mac[5],HEX);
Serial.print(":");
Serial.print(mac[4],HEX);
Serial.print(":");
Serial.print(mac[3],HEX);
Serial.print(":");
Serial.print(mac[2],HEX);
Serial.print(":");
Serial.print(mac[1],HEX);
Serial.print(":");
Serial.println(mac[0],HEX);
```

```
// printing subnet mask:
IPAddress subnet = WiFi.subnetMask();
Serial.print("NetMask: ");
Serial.println(subnet);
// printing gateway address:
IPAddress gateway = WiFi.gatewayIP();
Serial.print("Gateway: ");
Serial.println(gateway);
}
void printCurrentNet() {
// printing the SSID of the network you're connected to
Serial.print("SSID: ");
Serial.println(WiFi.SSID());
// printing the MAC address of the router you're connected to
byte bssid[6];
WiFi.BSSID(bssid);
Serial.print("BSSID: ");
Serial.print(bssid[5],HEX);
Serial.print(":");
Serial.print(bssid[4],HEX);
```

```
Serial.print(":");
Serial.print(bssid[3],HEX);
Serial.print(":");
Serial.print(bssid[2],HEX);
Serial.print(":");
Serial.print(bssid[1],HEX);
Serial.print(":");
Serial.println(bssid[0],HEX);
// printing signal strength
long rssi = WiFi.RSSI();
Serial.print("signal strength (RSSI):");
Serial.println(rssi);
// printing type of encryption
byte encryption = WiFi.encryptionType();
Serial.print("Encryption Type:");
Serial.println(encryption,HEX);
}
```

Once we import the WiFi library, we have to name our network. Make sure to change this name to your own, otherwise the program won't work. With that in mind, let's move on to our setup section. We need to instantiate a serial connection and perform a verification procedure to make sure that the module is connected. This is why we use the Wi-Fi status function. If it returns the WL_NO_SHIELD constant, it simply means that there's no module present, and an infinite loop will be executed to recheck periodically. The same function can also return different values, and we state that if anything other than WL_CONNECTED is received, we print an argument which informs the connection attempt. At this point the WiFi.begin function will perform connection attempts for as long as there is no connection detected. We also included a 10 second delay so that the connection attempt is performed in intervals instead of bombarding the system too aggressively. Once the connection is successful, we print a serial message which specifies the connection status as "connected." The last piece of the puzzle involves two functions that print all the components that are connected to the status of the network and its parameters. In order to learn more about these elements, you should consult the reference guide that comes with the WiFi library. Once the network connection is established, data can be exchanged between the device, however don't forget that in this example we aren't using any kind of encryption methods. Using Wi-Fi without any type of security system can be dangerous and risky, because anyone could have access to the network and extract your data packets.

Now that you have all the knowledge you need regarding networks and communications, you should consider implementing an encryption system as your homework. You can use the WiFi library to add these security functions, so make sure to give the library's reference a good read as it contains everything you need to know.

CONCLUSION

You have finished absorbing everything *Arduino Programming: The Ultimate Intermediate Guide to Learn Arduino Programming Step By Step* has to offer! Congratulations! Now you have everything you need to go out on your own and start building the projects of your dreams. You learned how to connect any kind of module in order to extend the functionality of the Arduino board, and now you can finally start building more complex projects, such as robots! Start taking over the world and share everything with other Arduino fans and extend your knowledge about electronics, computers, and programming.

Remember, if you feel intimidated by certain topics, or if you think you aren't that great at coding, you shouldn't give up! There's a solution for everything and there are many online communities out there willing to help. Explore the applications step by step, read more module datasheets and reference guides, examine project schematics, and start building! The things you can achieve with the Arduino are incredible, and you should continue practicing because nobody becomes an engineer or a developer overnight without practice.

Congratulations on continuing with the Arduino guide series and advancing to the next level! Keep this guide close, and continue expanding your knowledge with more books, more tutorials, and more practice. Start building your army of Arduino robots today and conquer the world, because why not?